21.

6

ON THE FIRST EDITION

OF THE

CHEMICAL WRITINGS

OF

DEMOCRITUS AND SYNESIUS:

FOUR PAPERS READ TO THE

PHILOSOPHICAL SOCIETY OF GLASGOW,

NOVEMBER, 1884—OCTOBER, 1894.

BY

JOHN FERGUSON, M.A., LL.D.,

F.R.S.E., F.S.A.LOND. & SCOT., F.C.S., &c.

REGIUS PROFESSOR OF CHEMISTRY IN THE UNIVERSITY; PRESIDENT OF THE
PHILOSOPHICAL SOCIETY AND OF THE ARCHÆOLOGICAL SOCIETY, GLASGOW.

GLASGOW:
PRINTED BY ROBERT ANDERSON, 22 ANN STREET.
1894.

III.—*On the First Editions of the Chemical Writings of Democritus and Synesius.* By JOHN FERGUSON, M.A., Professor of Chemistry in the University of Glasgow.

[Read before the Society, 19th November, 1884.]

1. DEMOCRITUS, the oldest known writer on chemical topics, is the nominal author of a tract in Greek, entitled Φυσικὰ καὶ Μυστικά, which is contained in most of the Greek alchemical Manuscripts.* Some of the older historians of chemistry tried to identify him with the Greek philosopher of the same name, but there is no evidence to support such a view. From a variety of considerations, however, it is probable that he flourished not later than the third or fourth century A.D., so that the subject about which he wrote cannot be considered an absolutely modern one. His curious tract has never been edited in the original language; its contents are known only through a Latin translation, executed in the sixteenth century by an Italian named Dominico Pizimenti. As no more ancient alchemical writer than Democritus is known, this writing of his would be of the greatest importance, were it not rendered almost useless by its obscurity. Familiar words and expressions are indeed constantly employed, but it is questionable if they have the meanings attached to them now, or carry the same meanings throughout the tract itself. The whole work bears the

---

* These manuscripts are described in full by Dr. Kopp in his great work; *Beiträge zur Geschichte der Chemie,* Braunschweig, 1869, 8vo, Parts i.-ii., which contains all that is at present known about the Greek alchemists and their writings. As the first portion of the present paper is simply an abridgment of Dr. Kopp's results, I make this reference to his work once for all, to avoid constant quotation. For the same reason I curtail reference to the older writers as much as possible, as they are all to be found in Dr. Kopp's notes. A paper by myself, giving a sketch of Dr. Kopp's researches and a list of the MSS., was printed in the *Proceedings* of this Society for 1876, vol. x., pp. 368-89. It is the existence of that paper which has induced me to submit to the Society the present communication also, one so entirely technical in detail and limited in interest, that it can appeal to only one or two specialists.

stamp of an esotericism, the aim and the interpretation of which are alike a puzzle to the historian.

2. Over and above the difficulty of interpretation, there is nearly as much in ascertaining precisely such apparently commonplace and obvious matters as the date when the translation was first printed, and the number of editions of it which appeared. Dr. Kopp, who has gone into these questions most minutely, has not been able to arrive at a definite settlement of them. In his survey of the statements made by the different authorities he has found them at such variance with one another that he has been constrained to believe that the descriptions of the various editions could not have been written from inspection of actual copies. As he himself has succeeded, after great trouble, in seeing a copy of only one edition, all that he has been able to do for the others has been to compare the statements of different writers, and to get from them what seem to be the best conclusions under the circumstances. Subsequent inquirers are under a deep obligation to him for the amount of labour he has thus spared them.

3. Of Pizimenti's translation, the number of editions quoted incidentally by Dr. Kopp from the various authorities is considerable. They are as follows:—Rome, 1570; Padua, 1572, 1573; Cologne, 1572, 1574; Frankfurt, 1592, 1613, 1673; Nürnberg, 1717.

For the edition of 1570 there is the authority of Conring. Dr. Kopp, however, attaches no importance to it; he does not criticise Conring's statement about it; he does not apparently think it worth while to consider even the possibility of its existence, for he looks upon this date as an error. I shall consider it below (§ 11).

The Padua edition of 1572 is mentioned by Ducange, by Grässe, and by Mullach. Dr. Kopp considers this date also erroneous.

It is the Padua edition of 1573 which is reckoned by him the first or oldest, and he gives the following title:—" Democritus Abderita de arte magna sive de rebus naturalibus; nec non Synesii et Pelagii, et Stephani Alexandrini et Mich. Pselli in eundem commentaria. Dom. Pizimentio Vibonensi interprete. Patavii, 1573.

After much searching and trouble, Dr. Kopp succeeded at last in finding a copy of this extremely rare book in the University Library at Göttingen; the very volume, I suppose, described by Beckmann, who was professor of Technology there towards the end of last century. The title and date of it are given with actual or approximate accuracy by Fabricius, Hoffmann, Beckmann, Brunet, and Grässe; but Dr. Kopp has adduced abundant evidence to show how very scarce the book is, and how little it is known.

4. The next edition to be considered is that contained in a Cologne reprint of the treatise on Secrets by Antoine Mizauld, entitled: *Memorabilium . . . Centuriæ Novem.* About the date of this book much confusion prevails. Dr. Kopp, who himself has not seen any Cologne edition, has compared all that has been said by the different authorities, but has given up the attempt to reconcile their conflicting statements. The following are the two chief points:—

(1) Both Fabricius and Lambeck say that it appeared at Cologne in 1572. Believing, as he does, that the Padua edition of 1573 is the oldest, Dr. Kopp feels naturally very sceptical about one of 1572, and remarks that if one there be, in all probability it is of a different translation from Pizimenti's.

(2) Reinesius—followed by Dufresnoy, Hoffmann, Gmelin, and Schmieder—quotes an edition of 1574 only. Conring, who, as mentioned above, says that the translation first appeared in 1570, adds that it was reprinted at Cologne four years later, thus indirectly confirming the statement of Reinesius.

5. Besides the 1574 edition just mentioned, Dufresnoy quotes the following:—Frankfurt, 1592, 1613 and 1673, but without saying definitely whether these are reprints of Mizauld's and Democritus' tracts, or of Democritus' alone. If he mean that these are joint editions, Dr. Kopp points out that copies of Mizauld, Frankfurt, 1592, 1599, and 1613, which he has examined, do not contain Democritus. I have likewise examined a copy of the 1592 edition, and can confirm Dr. Kopp's statement with regard to it. As to the edition of 1673, Dr. Kopp does not speak, he apparently not having seen it. If, however, Dufresnoy mean the latter, Dr. Kopp has been equally unsuccessful in seeing copies of Pizimenti's translation by itself, printed at Frankfurt and having any of these dates.

Schmieder is more definite than Dufresnoy, but he is probably on that account more inaccurate. He gives the title of the Padua edition, 1573, and adds immediately: " the same text was copied in the newer editions: Coloniæ, 1574, 16.; Francofurti, 1592, 1613, 1673, 8." Here no notice is taken of Mizauld's book at all, and one would be led to believe that these were reprints of

Democritus alone, from the Padua edition direct. All this seems to me very doubtful; if there be a Cologne 1574 edition it is most likely a reprint of Mizauld with Democritus; while of the other dates, the only copies known want Democritus. My own opinion is that the editions of 1592, 1613, 1673, need not be taken into account until actual copies of Mizauld with Democritus, or until separate editions of Democritus alone with these dates be discovered, an event which I think will never happen.

6. The last edition mentioned by Dr. Kopp is that printed at Nürnberg, in 1717. He himself has not seen it, but he quotes it from Hoffmann, and observes that its title is different from that of 1573. It is very remarkable, as showing the doubt hanging round the whole subject, that even respecting this almost modern edition there is contradiction, for while Hoffmann gives the title in Latin, Dufresnoy, and after him Schmieder, say that it was in German. Dr. Kopp is unable to decide who is right.

7. It would appear, therefore, as if, of the several editions mentioned during the last three centuries, only one—that of Padua, 1573—were properly authenticated by competent authorities, Beckmann and Dr. Kopp.

The foregoing summary is requisite for the proper understanding of what I have discovered lately on this subject.

8. In the course of certain researches, not immediately concerned with Democritus, I was led recently to investigate Mizauld's *Memorabilium Centuriae Novem*, of which a copy of the Frankfurt edition, 1592, had come into my hands (§ 5). Looking for other editions, I found first in Sir William Hamilton's Collection, now in the University Library, and, thereafter, in the Hunterian Library, copies of Mizauld's work printed at Cologne in 1572. On examining the two copies, I observed that they both contained the tract of Democritus, with the commentaries, translated by Pizimenti. The following is a detailed description of the book :—

Title: Antonii Mizaldi Mon- | luciani Galli, Medici, | Memorabi- | livm, Sive Arca- | norvm omnis Ge- | neris, | Per Aphorismos Di- | gestorum, Centuriæ IX. | Et, | Democritvs Abderita, De | rebus Naturalibus & Mysticis. | Cum | Synesii, et Pelagii | Commentarijs. | Interprete' de Græca lingua, | Dominico Pizimentio Vibonen- | si, Italo. | Præfatio, | In omnes hosce libros. | Coloniæ, | Apud Ioannem Birckmannum | Anno D.M.LXXII. | Cum Gratia & Priuilegio Cæsar. Maiestat. |

5 2/16 × 3 1/16 inches. Signatures in twelves; ff. 52 unnumbered and 2 blank, 245 numbered, 1 blank. Printed in italics.

Collation:—f. 2 recto: De Mizaldi | Arcanis, Nec Non | Graecis in Demo |
critvm, Ceteris- | què, Chemiæ scripto- | ribus, | Præfatio, | Ad Clar-
issimvm No- | bilitate, doctrina, prudentiaquè virum, | Thomam
Redingervm | Silesivm. |

This preface ends on f. 32 r. with the words: comparatur. Vale.
Calen- | dis Martijs. M.D. | LXXII. Vbio- | rum Colo- | nia. | (∵) |
followed by a scroll ornament. On f. 32 v. begins Iudex Rervm,
which ends on f. 51 v. Then follows f. 52 r. Praefationis errores
incvria ad- | missos, sic corrige. | *ending f. 52 v. Ff. 53 and 54 are
blank. This ends the introductory matter which is not numbered. The
text of Mizaldus' treatise then begins on leaf A, f. 1, and goes down to the
recto of f. 212. Verso is blank.*

F. 213 contains the title to the chemical tracts as follows:—

Ex | Venerandæ Græcæ vetustatis de ar- | te Chymica, relliqnijs(sic). |
Democritvs | Abderyta, De Arte | Sacra: Sive, De Rebvs | naturalibus
& my- | sticis | Necnon | Synesij, & Pelagij, Antiquorum | Philoso-
phorum: in eundem, ⊢ Commentaria. | Interprete | Dominico Pizimentio
Vibo- | nens, Italo. *Small scroll ornament.*

*F. 213 verso is blank. F. 214 recto contains Pizimenti's preface, which ends
f. 218 recto with the words:* Stephani Alexandrini, Olympiodori, | &
Pelagii cōmentaria, in eundem | Democritum propediem ex- | pecta.
Datum Romę. | Calend. Septemb. | M.D.LXX. | (∵) | *The catchword
is* Ex. *Then f. 218 v. begins:* De Rebvs Na- | tvralibvs et My- | sticis
Demo- | criti. | Natvra natura | gaudet: &c., *which ends f. 227 verso:*
omisi, | cùm liberè in alijs etiam | meis scriptis pertractarim. | In hoc
scripto | valete. | (∵)

F. 228 recto: Synesii Phi- | losophi ad Dio- | scorvm in Librvm | Democriti.
| Scholia. | *with a scroll ornament. It ends f. 238 verso.*

F 239 recto: Pelagii Pbilo- | sophi De Eadem | Divina, et Sacra | arte. |
Ends f. 245 verso. A blank leaf ends the volume.

Two things follow of necessity from this description: 1°,
the Padua edition of 1573 cannot be the first, as Dr. Kopp with
the materials at his command quite legitimately inferred; 2°,
Dr. Kopp's supposition that if there were an edition prior to that
of Padua, 1573, it could not have been one of Pizimenti's translation, is disposed of by the statements on the title-pages.

9. Pursuing my researches still further, I found in the British
Museum no copy of the 1572 edition, but another printed also at
Cologne by Birckmann, in the following year, 1573. I at first
thought that this might be simply a re-issue of the remainder of
the previous edition, with a new or re-dated title-page. On
examination, however, I found this was not the case, but that it
was a veritably new edition. As it is entirely unknown, and has

never been mentioned by any writer on the subject, the following
account of it may be given :—

Title: Antonii Mizaldi Mon- | luciani Galli, Medici, | Memorabilivm, Sive
Arca- | norvm omnis ge- | neris, | Per Aphorismos Di- | gestorum, Cen-
turiæ IX. | Et | Democritvs Abderita, De | rebus Naturælibus, &
Mysticis. | Cum | Synesii, et Pelagii | Commentarijs. | Interprete de
Græca lingua, | Dominico Pziimentio Vibonen- | si, Italo. | Præfatio, |
In omnes hosce libros. | Coloniae, | apud Ioannem Birckmannum |
. Anno. D.M.LXXIII. | Cum Gratia & Priuilegio Cæsar. Maiestat. |
5 ²/₁₆ by 2 ¹²/₁₆ *inches. Signatures in twelves: ff. 45 unnumbered, 245
numbered. Printed in italics.*

Folio 2 recto: De Mizaldi Arcanis...Præfatio, *ends f. 31 verso. Folio 32
recto:* Index Rerum *to f. 45 recto. 45 verso is blank. There is no
table of Errata. The text begins on A, f. 1, and goes down to f. 212
recto. Verso is blank.*

Fol. 213 recto: Ex | Venerandæ Græcæ vetustatis de ar- | te Chymica,
relliquijs (*sic*). | Democritvs | Abderyta, de Arte | sacra: Sive, De Rebvs
| naturalibus & my- | sticis, | Necnon | Synesij, & Pelagij, Antiquorum
| Philosophorum : in eundem, | Commentaria. | Interprete | Dominico
Pizimentio Vibo- | nensi Italo. | *Small scroll ornament.*

Folio 214 recto: Pizimenti's address, *which ends f. 218 recto:* Romæ, Calend.
Septemb. M.D.LXX.

Folio 218 verso: Ex Rebvs Na- | tvralibvs et My- | sticis Demo- | criti.

Folio 228 recto: Synesii Phi | losophi ad Dio- | scorvm in Librvm |
Democriti. | Scholia, (∵) | *followed by large scroll ornament.*

Folio 239 recto: Pelagii Philo- | sophi de eadem | Divina et Sacra | arte (∵)
| *ends f. 245 verso.*

Comparison of these two editions shows that, though identical in
some points, they differ materially in others ; for example, in the
preliminary matter, which occupies 52 ff. in one copy, and 45 ff. in
the other; in the absence of a table of errata in the 1573 edition,
and in many details of typography, which show that the type
must have been taken down and set up again before the 1573
edition was printed off.

10. The discovery of these two editions, however, has more important bearings. It introduces new difficulties, and makes the
construction of a complete and authoritative list by no means so
simple as at first sight appears.

Seeing that the edition of Padua (1573) has to cede the first
place to that of Cologne (1572), a difficulty is created thereby
which cannot, with our present knowledge, be well got over.

It seems to me rather improbable that a translation by an
Italian should be published for the first time at Cologne. It

seems equally improbable that it should appear as an appendix to a quite different work by a Frenchman, which had been published at Paris six years earlier. I cannot help thinking it likely that there must have been an earlier edition printed, one would expect, in Italy. Two such are mentioned.

Ducange, as has been seen above, quotes a Padua edition of 1572. He never saw it, however, and could not tell whether it was in Greek or in Latin. Dr. Kopp, knowing only the Padua edition of 1573, naturally enough considers this to be an error of Ducange, but I am not at all sure that it is so. It seems just as likely that there were two editions at Padua in 1572, 1573, as that there were two at Cologne in 1572, 1573, both of which I have seen and just described. If so, it is reasonable to suppose that the Padua edition of 1572 was the earlier; but in that case Birckmann must have got a copy before March 1, 1572. For in his preface, which has that date, he says that when he had got half through the printing of Mizaldus' book, Joannes Metellus Sequanus sent him the tracts of Democritus and the others, and requested them to be added, which he did. Now, Sequanus is the person to whom Pizimenti addresses his translation from Rome on September 1st, 1570. The question then arises—Was the copy which Sequanus sent printed or manuscript? Birckmann does not say; but as he does say that he got Mizaldus' book also from Sequanus, we may assume that it was a printed copy, probably of the Paris edition, 1566. It is plausible to infer that the other was also printed.

11. The evidence in favour of the *possibility* of such an earlier edition is twofold—First, There is the date of Pizimenti's translation just referred to : Rome, Sept. 1st, 1570. If finished then, it would be curious if it was not printed till Sequanus sent the MS. to Birckmann, who brought it out in 1572. But if that be so, there may be possibly no Padua edition of 1572 at all, and that of 1573 may be a reprint from Birckmann's.

Secondly, Conring, as has been already mentioned, speaks of a 1570 edition at Rome:—" Supersunt verò ijdem illi Democritei libelli hodieque; ἀνέκδοτοι tamen hactenus, nisi quod unum eorum cum Synesii & Pelagii scholiis Latinè à se versum, Romæ seculi superioris anno septuagesimo ediderit Dominicus Pizimentius; quam editionem in Germania quarto anno pòst Coloniæ Agrippinæ cum Mizaldi Memorabilibus alii expresserunt."[*]

---

[*] De Hermetica Medicina. 1669. p. 29.

This seems precise enough; the originals remain unpublished hitherto, excepting that Pizimenti published at Rome in 1570 a Latin translation of one of them, which was reprinted four years later at Cologne. There is certainly no evidence here of Conring having seen a copy, and he may be merely inferring from the date of the dedication that there was an edition of 1570. I do not know of the existence of any copy of this date, but there is nothing against it when there is so much doubt as to the date of the first edition.

12. As for a 1574 Cologne edition, we have the word of Reinesius, of Conring, and other later writers, already quoted. I have seen no copy, and no mention of one in any catalogue. Its existence, however, is quite possible.

Of the reprint of Mizaldus, Frankfurt, 1592, I have already spoken. It does not contain Democritus. The reprints of 1599, 1613 certainly, and of 1673 probably, do not contain it, and there is no proof that there are separate editions of Democritus with these dates.

13. Nothing more was heard of Democritus till the year 1717, when the tract was reprinted. Dr. Kopp has failed to see it; but I have been more successful, and the following is a description of the copy I have had before me:—

Title (printed in red and black): Democritus | Abderyta Græcus | De | Rebus Sacris | Naturalibus et Mysticis. | Cum Notis | Synesii & Pelagii. | Tumba | Semiramidis | Hermeticæ *(sic)* Sigillatæ, | Quàm | Si Sapiens aperuerit, | Non | Cyrus, Ambitiosus; | Avarus, | Regum ille thesauros, divitiarum inexhaustos, | quod sufficiat inveniet. | H.V.D. | Norimbergæ, |. Apud Hæredes Joh. Dan. Tauberi, | M.DCC.XVII. |

Small 8vo, pp. 63, and a page of advertisements.

Pizimenti's Preface, p. 3; Democritus, p. 10; Synesius, p. 19; Pelagius, p. 32, ending p. 38; after which comes the Tumba Semiramidis.

This is a reprint of the Latin. Dufresnoy says, in so many words, that it is in German, and Schmieder makes the same assertion, either of his own knowledge or following Dufresnoy. I am unable to say whether there be a German translation of this date or not. There is nothing impossible in the book appearing simultaneously in both languages, but the statement may also have arisen from confusing the two tracts ascribed to Synesius, as I shall show presently. Dr. Kopp does not express any opinion.

After 1717 the book passed into oblivion, so far as I know, until Dr. Kopp reprinted it in his *Beiträge* in 1869, from the Padua edition of 1573. This reprint was confined to Democritus.

14. The list of editions to which this research has conducted me is rather larger than what Dr. Kopp has been able to muster. It is as follows:—

Date.		Place.				Authority.
1570 (?),	...	Rome (?),	...	...	...	Conring.
1572,	...	Cologne,	.,	...	...	Ferguson.
1572 (?),	...	Padua (?),	...	...	...	Ducange.
1573,	...	Cologne (previously unknown),				Ferguson.
1573,	...	Padua, ...	...	...	...	Beckmann, Kopp.
1574 (?),	...	Cologne (?),	...	...	...	Reinesius, Conring.
1717,	...	Nürnberg (in Latin),			...	Ferguson.
1717 (?),	...	Nürnberg (?) (in German),		...		Dufresnoy, Schmieder.
1869,	...	Braunschweig,		...	...	Reprint in Kopp's *Beiträge.*

15. Everyone who has examined the Φυσικὰ καὶ Μυστικά has been compelled to give up the interpretation of it. It is obscure in the highest degree; the only thing that seems tolerably certain is that it deals with transmutation. *How* transmutation is to be effected it does not tell us, or if it does, it is in language which we cannot interpret. Indeed, we cannot form any idea of how the writer regarded the problem.

This obscurity seems to have been felt at a very early date, for the next oldest extant chemical writing is the commentary by Synesius, professing to explain the Democritean philosophy. It need hardly be added that, like other works of the same kind, it is as obscure as the original.

Regarding the author's life, the age of the commentary, the absence of an edition of the Greek text, the editions of Pizimenti's translation, everything that has been said about Democritus may be repeated. The older writers tried to identify Synesius with the Bishop of the same name, but that is undoubtedly wrong. The author of this commentary was subsequent to him by an interval, possibly by a wide interval, of time.

Of the writing itself we know only through Pizimenti's translation, and as it accompanies Democritus' tract in the actual editions of Cologne 1572 and 1573, Padua 1573, and Nürnberg 1717, it is most probable that if any of the doubtful editions exist the tract of Synesius will be contained in them. Dr. Kopp has not reprinted this commentary.

16. But there is another point of interest connected with Synesius. A tract, purporting to be by him, was printed in the modern languages.

In a foot-note (*Beiträge*, p. 151, nr. 28) Dr. Kopp says :—

"Giebt es auch Uebersetzungen in's Englische und in's Deutsche ? Wo Fabricius (Bibl. gr., vol. xii., p. 769) der lateinischen Uebersetzung des Pizimenti erwähnt, fügt er bei : Ejusdem argumenti scriptum Synesianum ex codice bibl. caesarea versum anglice exstat ad calcem Basilii Valentini in anglicam conversi linguam Lond. 1678 et germanice curante Frid. Rothscholzio Altdorf 1718. Ich kann beide hier citirte Schriften nicht nachsehen."

I have been again more lucky than Dr. Kopp, for I have not only seen these two editions, but I have seen no fewer than nine editions, including a number in French, which Dr. Kopp has somehow missed.

The French is the oldest edition of the work I am acquainted with. It appeared at Paris in 1612, in a thin 4to volume, along with the works of Artephius and Flamel, under the title: *Trois Traictez de la Philosophie Natvrelle, non encore imprimez,* translated by P. Arnauld. I have seen three copies having this date; two are alike, the third is different, so that there must have been two issues of this book. One issue contains pp. 103; the tract of Synesius occupying pp. 94–103. The other contains pp. 98; the tract of Synesius occupying pp. 89–98. In 1659 there appeared a new edition of the second issue. Finally, it was included in the collection of alchemical tracts, entitled *Bibliotheque des Philosophes Chimiques,* published at Paris, 1740–41, tom. ii., pp. 175–194. The English translation was printed at London in 1678. Though appended to Basil Valentine's *Triumphant Chariot of Antimony,* it has a separate title-page: *The True Book of the learned Synesius, a Greek abbot, taken out of the Emperour's Library, concerning the Philosopher's Stone.* It was probably translated by Richard Russell. It was reprinted at London by Francis Barrett in his curious collection of alchemical tracts so recently as 1815.

The German version was executed by Roth-Scholtz, and was printed, along with the works of Sendivogius, at Nürnberg, in 1718 by the heirs of Joh. Dan. Tauber. It will have been observed that the 1717 edition of Democritus and Synesius was printed by the same people, and indeed it is advertised at the end of this translation. It is possible that the statement by Dufresnoy and by Schmieder respecting a German translation of Democritus and

Synesius in 1717 may be due to confusing the two tracts of Synesius, and then assuming that Democritus had also been translated. This is mere supposition, however. Synesius was included in the translation of Flamel's works by Johann Lange, of which I have seen two editions printed at Vienna—one dated 1751, and the other 1752.

17. The fact is, however, that what passes under the name of Synesius in these modern versions is not the Commentary on Democritus, edited by Pizimenti. Whether by Synesius or not, it is a totally different production, and, as the name of Geber occurs in it, it may doubted if the tract is of any great antiquity, or if we have got it in a form devoid of recent interpolations. One noticeable thing about it is that there is no version of it in Latin, so far as I know; for Dr. Kopp's remark, above quoted, rests on the supposition that the English and German translations are from Pizimenti's version, which is not the case. I am not in a position to say anything at present about the origin and author of these works; they must wait until the two ancient writers whom we have been considering are better known.

18. Corresponding to the list of the Democritus editions already given, the following for Synesius may be useful:—

COMMENTARY ON DEMOCRITUS.

Date.			Place.
1572,	...	...	Cologne.
1573,	...	...	Cologne.
1573,	...	...	Padua.
1717,	...	...	Nürnberg.

For the doubtful editions, see §§ 5 and 14.

"THE TRUE BOOK."

French—1612,	...	Paris.		
1612,	...	Paris.	...	2nd issue.
1659,	...	Paris.	...	
1740,	...	Paris.	...	Richebourg's Collection.
German—1718,	...	Nürnberg.		With Sendivogius.
1751,	...	Vienna.	...	With Flamel.
1752,	...	Vienna.	...	With Flamel.
English—1678,	...	London.	...	With B. Valentine.
1815,	...	London.	...	Barrett's Collection.

On the First Editions of the Chemical Writings of Democritus and Synesius. By Professor FERGUSON.

POSTSCRIPT.

1. IN consequence of my not having beside me the copy of the 1573 edition of Mizauld's *Memorabilia*, when the account of it given in § 9 was printed, two or three mistakes have slipped in, which I take this opportunity of correcting.

In the third line of the title, the word "Memorabilivm" ought to be divided "Memorabi- | livm," as in the 1572 edition, § 8.

In the sixteenth line of the title, "Pziimentio" ought, of course, to be "Pizimentio."

Lastly, in the twentieth and twenty-first lines, "Coloniae, | apud" ought to be "Coloniae. | Apud"

2. In § 15 it is said that there is no edition of the Greek text of the Commentary on Democritus by Synesius. This is an error. It was printed by Fabricius, with Pizimenti's Latin translation, in the *Bibliotheca Græca*, Hamb. 1717, vol. viii., pp. 233-248.

3. A translation of this Commentary into German was made by Dr. Fried. Jos. Willh. Schröder, and was printed in his *Neue Sammlung der Bibliothek für die höhere Naturwissenschaft und Chemie*, Leipzig, 1775. It occupies pp. 431-454, and its title is as follows:—

Die hieroglyfischen Fragmente des Demokritus; oder des Egyptiers Synesius Commentar über die Bücher des Demokritus von der Tinctur des Goldes und Silbers; an den Priester Dioskorus.

In a note Schröder warns his readers not to confuse this Synesius and the "Commentary" with the supposititious abbot Synesius and the "True Book" which passes under his name. In this he is without doubt correct. He says, however, that the "Commentary" is the oldest genuine Greek alchemical tract extant, and that the author flourished 250 years B.C. In this he is without doubt wrong.

4. Of the "True Book" itself I have met with other two editions.

In 1682 P. Arnauld's collection was re-issued with the following title-page:—

Philosophie Natvrelle de Trois Anciens Philosophes Renommez Artephius, Flamel, & Synesius, Traitant de l'Art occulte, & de la Transmutation metallique.   Derniere edition.   Augmentée d'un petit Traité du Mercure, & de la Pierre des Philosophes de G. Ripleus, nouvellement traduit en François.   A Paris, Chez Laurent d'Houry, sur le Quay des Augustins, à l'Image Saint Jean.   M.DC.LXXXII.   Avec Privilege dv Roy.

It is a thin 4to of 106 pages.   *Le Vray Livre* of Synesius occupies pp. 89-98, and at the foot of p. 98 is the date, *6 Avril, 1659*.   So that, although professing to be a new edition, this seems to be merely the surplus copies of the edition of 1659, to which Ripley's tract has been added and a new title-page prefixed.

5. The German translation of Flamel and Synesius by J. Lange (§16) was first printed at Hamburg, "In Verlegung Adolph Härtels, Anno 1681."   In this edition there are two titles; the first, which is printed in red and black, is dated 1681; the second, 1680.   The translation of Synesius is contained in pp. 89-109.

These different books, which I have recently examined in the British Museum, fall to be inserted in their proper places in the list of editions of Synesius given in § 18.

6. In § 8, in the twentieth line of the title of Mizauld's work, "Coloniæ" ought to have been printed "Coloniae."

GLASGOW, *May 8th, 1885.*

Philosophical Society of Glasgow.

REMARKS ON THE FIRST EDITION

OF THE

CHEMICAL WRITINGS

OF

DEMOCRITUS AND SYNESIUS.

PART II.

BY

Professor JOHN FERGUSON,

LL.D., F.R.S.E., F.S.A., F.S.A.Scot.

READ BEFORE THE GLASGOW PHILOSOPHICAL SOCIETY,
19TH NOVEMBER, 1890.

GLASGOW:
PRINTED BY ROBERT ANDERSON, 22 ANN STREET.

[FROM THE *PROCEEDINGS* OF THE PHILOSOPHICAL SOCIETY OF GLASGOW.]

Remarks on the First Edition of the Chemical Writings of Democritus and Synesius. Part II. By Professor JOHN FERGUSON, LL.D., F.R.S.E., F.S.A., F.S.A.Scot.

[Read before the Society, 19th November, 1890.]

1. The paper on this subject which I communicated to the Society on Nov. 19, 1884, exactly six years ago, was occasioned by my having seen an edition of Democritus, dated a year earlier than that of Padua, 1573, which is considered by Dr. Kopp, the chief authority on the subject, as the first. This edition, published at Cologne by Johann Birckmann in 1572, appended to Mizaldus' *Memorabilia*, of which I had discovered copies in the Hunterian and University Libraries here, was fully described in the paper, and it was also pointed out that the existence of it necessarily involved important modifications in the opinions advanced as to the date and place of the first publication of the book.

In the same paper there was described another edition, dated 1573, also published at Cologne by Johann Birckmann, a copy of which I had found in the British Museum. This was new, for no previous writer about Democritus, so far as I am aware, makes any allusion to it whatsoever. It is a reprint of the previous edition, and is exactly like it in size, type, and arrangement, so much so that one might have supposed it to be an issue of remainder copies with a re-dated title page, but a cursory examination showed that the two editions were typographically different from end to end, and that the 1573 is a veritably new edition.

2. The Cologne 1572 edition just mentioned was not absolutely

unknown. It had been referred to by Fabricius and Lambeccius,[*] but in so vague a way that Dr. Kopp, who knew only the Padua edition of 1573, and believed it to be the first, felt justified in questioning the existence of such an edition altogether. But the discovery of two copies here, and the subsequent examination of a copy by Dr. Kopp himself, as he informed me, put an end to the possibility of doubt on the matter.[†]

3. Notwithstanding the existence of an edition of 1572, and reference to it by certain authorities, it appears to have been so rare that it was hardly known. That of 1573 is still rarer, for it is not mentioned at all. At all events both were unknown to Reinesius,[‡] who mentions an edition of Cologne 1574 only, but in a very vague way. This last is, indeed, confirmed indirectly by Conring, who, speaking of the work, says that it first appeared at Rome in 1570, and was reprinted four years later at Cologne. But as his initial statement requires the strongest of all confirmations, namely, the existence of an actual copy dated Rome, 1570, his somewhat loose remark that the book appeared four years later might not be meant to be interpreted quite strictly. When, therefore, I said[§] that the existence of a 1574 edition was quite possible, although I had seen no copy anywhere mentioned, it seemed to me so barely probable that an edition of Mizaldus' Secrets, with Democritus and Synesius appended, should appear at Cologne in three successive years, 1572, 1573, 1574, by the same printer, Birckmann, that I did not feel justified in removing the query from the 1574 edition in the list which I gave.[||]

4. Here again I have been shown by facts the error of a too sweeping doubt, for I have within the last week ascertained that a copy of the work, dated 1574, is in the University Library at Cambridge, and by the kindness of the librarian, Mr. Jenkinson, I have been able to examine it, and compare it with the edition of 1572.

---

[*] *Proceedings of the Philosophical Society of Glasgow*, 1885. Vol. xvi., p. 38.

[†] March, 1891.—I have since seen another copy of the 1572 edition of Mizaldus in the Library of Trinity College, Cambridge.

[‡] *Ibid.*, p. 38.   [§] *Ibid.*, p. 43.   [||] *Ibid.*, p. 44.

The following is a description of this volume similar to what I gave of the 1572 edition in the previous paper (§ 9).

5.

ANTONII MIZALDI MON-
luciani Galli, Medici,

MEMORABI-
LIVM, SIVE ARCA-
NORVM OMNIS GE-
NERIS,

PER APHORISMOS DI-
geftorum, Centuriæ IX.

ET

DEMOCRITVS ABDERITA, DE
rebus Naturalibus, & Myfticis.

Cum

SYNESII, ET PELAGII

Commentarijs.

Interprete de Græca lingua,
Dominico Pizimentio Vibanen-
fi Italo.

Præfatio,

In omnes hofce libros.

COLONIAE,

Apud Ioannem Birckmannum
Anno D.M.LXXIIII.

Cum Gratia & Priuilegio Cæfar. Maieftat.

24°. *Signatures in 12.* * Title ; * 2r to ***7v [or 30 leaves] Præfatio *to Thomas Redinger, dated :* Calendis Martijs. M.D.LXXII. Vbiorum Colonia. ***8r to ****9r [or 14 leaves] Index Rerum præcipuarum. ****10, 11, 12, *are blank in this copy. The title and preliminary matter, therefore, occupy 48 leaves [3 blank] not numbered.*
The text is numbered consecutively from f. 1 to f. 245, or sigs. A to X6 in 12's. Text stops on X5 v. X6 is blank.

Collation : f. 1 : Title; *f.* 2 *recto :* De Mizaldi | Arcanis, Nec Non | Graecis In Demo- | critvm, Caeteris- | que Chemiæ scripto- | ribus, | Præfatio. | Ad Clarissimum No- | bilitate, doctrina, prudentiaque virum, | Thomam Redingervm | Silesivm. |

This preface ends on ***7v. or f. 31v. with the words: compara- | tur.
Vale. Calendis | Martijs. M.D. | LXXII.Vbio | rum Colo- | niæ | (·. ·)
| *with no scroll ornament.* On ****8r or f. 32r begins* Index Rervm,
*which ends on ****9r or f. 45 recto. Verso is blank, and three blank
leaves follow, completing the signature. This ends the introductory
matter, which is not numbered. The text of Mizaldus' treatise then
begins on leaf* A, *f.* 1, *and goes down to the recto of f.* 212. *Verso is
blank.*

F. 213r contains the title to the Chemical Tracts as follows :—

Ex | Venerandæ Græcæ vetustatis de ar- | te Chymica, relliquijs.
| Democritvs | Abderyta, De Arte | Sacra : Sive, De Rebvs | naturali-
bus & my- | sticis, | Necnon | Synesij, & Pelagij, Antiquorum
| Philosophorum : in eundem, | Commentaria. | Interprete | Dominico
Pizimentio Vibo- | nensi Italo. | *Small scroll ornament, same as in the
1572 edition. F.* 213 *verso is blank. F.* 214 *recto contains Pizimenti's
preface, which ends f.* 218 *recto, with the words :* Stephani Alexandrini,
Olympiodori, | & Pelagij cōmentaria, in eundem | Democritum pro-
pediem ex | pecta. Datum Romæ. | Calend. Septemb. | M.D.LXX.
| (·. ·) | *The catch word is* Ex. *Then F.* 218 *verso begins :* Ex Rebus Na-
| tvralibvs Et My- | sticis Demo- | criti. | (·. ·) | Natvra naturâ |
gaudet : *&c., which ends f.* 227 *verso :* omisi, cùm liberè in alijs etiam
| meis scriptis pertracta- | rim. In hoc scripto | valete. | (·. ·) |

F. 228 *recto :* Synesii Phi | losophi Ad Dio- | scorvm In Librvm
| Democriti. | Scholia, | (·. ·) | *with a scroll ornament, but quite
different from that in the edition of 1572. It ends f.* 238 *verso.*

F. 239 *recto :* Pelagii Philo- | sophi De Eadem | Divina Et Sacra
| arte. | (·. ·) | *Ends f.* 245 *verso, followed by a similar scroll ornament
to that on f.* 228, *whereas the ornament in the 1572 edition is the same as
that on f.* 228 *of the same edition. A blank leaf ends the volume.*

6. Comparison of this edition with that of 1572 shows, as
was to be expected, that they are absolutely different throughout.
The following are the main differences :—the 1572 edition con-
tains signatures *, **, ***, ****, all in twelves, ***** in six ; of
this last sheet the fourth leaf contains Errata, and 5 and 6 are
blank. A to X6 in twelves, X6 being blank.

The 1574 edition contains signatures *, **, ***, ****, all in
twelves ; this last sheet contains no Errata, and leaves 10, 11 and
12 are blank. A to X6 in twelves, X6 being blank.

In the 1572 edition, therefore, there are six leaves more than
in that of 1574, but the distinction between them is much greater
than that, for they differ typographically throughout.

7. But as regards the relationship of the 1573 and 1574 editions
I am not as yet certain, until I am able to compare this 1574

copy with that of 1573 in the British Museum.* As far as the account of the latter which I have already given [*Proceedings, Phil. Soc., Glasgow,* 1885, vol. **xvi.**, p. 40, § 9] shows, the 1574 edition is identical with it, except in the date. It is possible, therefore, that the 1574 is merely an issue of surplus copies of the previous year, with a re-dated title page, but I would not say so positively without careful comparison. It is just as possible that the edition of 1574 is really new, a reprint, differing typographically from those of 1572 and 1573, as that the edition of 1573 is quite different from that of 1572.

8. Anyhow, the existence of an edition dated 1574 is demonstrated by an actual copy of it.† The statements, therefore, of Reinesius and Conring as to a 1574 edition are justified, and the query appended to that edition in the list I have given [*Proceedings, Phil. Soc., Glasgow,* vol. **xvi.**, p. 44, § 14] may be deleted.

9. The discovery of this copy is of interest as showing how great the demand for these books must have been, when, in three successive years, 1572, 1573, 1574, there were three issues of them from the press of Birckmann at Cologne, two of which certainly are different from each other. It also gives a fresh illustration of the great rarity of all these books, when of them, one, that of 1573, was quite unknown until I described it, and I know now only one copy of it ; that of 1572 was denied by Dr. Kopp, and I know of only three or four copies of it ; while that of 1574 was questioned by me because the authorities for it appeared themselves to be vague as to its existence.

10. The preceding was all I had to put before the Society when I gave notice of these remarks as supplementary to my former paper ; but since then, only yesterday, I received the very interesting information that in the Cambridge University Library

---

[* I was not able to make this comparison till February, 1891. I have given the results at the end of the present paper.]

† March, 1891.—I have since ascertained that there is a copy of the 1574 edition in the University Library, Aberdeen, which, by the kindness of the librarian, I have been able to examine.

there is a copy of the edition of Democritus and Synesius printed
at Padua in 1573. This was the edition described by Beckmann,*
from the copy in the Göttingen University Library. It was also
the only edition of the work which Dr. Kopp† had before him in
1867, and which, after many inquiries, he, too, found at last in
Göttingen. At the time he considered this the first edition, those
of Cologne and Padua, dated 1572, being entirely doubted by him.
It was described by Fabricius and other later historians and
bibliographers, but it is doubtful if any of them ever saw a copy
of the edition. So that, as I formerly showed,‡ its existence was
authenticated by Beckmann at the end of last century, and by
Dr. Kopp twenty years ago, both of them using the same copy.
It was from this that Dr. Kopp made the reprint in his
Beiträge.

The following is a description of the copy in the University
Library, Cambridge :—

> Democritvs | Abderita | De Arte | Magna, | Siue de rebus naturalibus.
> | Nec non Synesii & Pelagii, & Stepha- | ni Alexandrini, et Michaelis
> Psel- | li in eundem commentaria. | Dominico Pizimentio Vibonensi
> | Interprete. | [*Device.*] | Patavii | Apud Simonem Galignanum |
> MDLXXIII. |

> It is a small octavo volume, signatures a to i, or 70 numbered leaves and 2
> blank leaves. The collation is as follows :—a1, title ; a2 recto to a5
> recto, or ff. 2 recto to 5 recto, Pizimenti's address to Cardinal Antonius
> Perenottus ; a5 verso, the text begins, and ends i6 recto, or ff. 5 verso
> to 70 verso ; i7 and 8 are blank leaves. The device on the title-page
> is an anchor enwreathed by a serpent, and grasped by two right
> hands issuing from clouds.

11. It is of excessive rarity. This is the only copy I know
of in this country, and the Göttingen one seems to be the only
known copy in Germany. There is no copy in the British Museum,
Bodleian, or any other library I have been able to examine.
Every writer who has spoken of it has emphasised its rarity.
I am, therefore, very fortunate in being able so unexpectedly to
add to my present communication an account from an actual copy

---

* *Beiträge zur Geschichte der Erfindungen*, Leipzig, 1792, III., p. 376 ; in
the English translation, London, 1814, III., p. 66.

† *Beiträge zur Geschichte der Chemie*, Braunschweig, 1867, p. 113, note 22.

‡ *Proceedings of the Philosophical Society of Glasgow*, 1885, vol. xvi.,
p. 37, § 3.

of this so rare book, the principal one, too, connected with the subject.

12. The existence of two independent editions, so to speak, —that of Cologne, 1572, and of Padua, 1573—makes me more than ever inclined to believe in the possibility of an earlier edition printed in Italy than any of those yet described. Two there may be—Rome, 1570, mentioned by Conring, which is the earliest possible, and Padua, 1572, mentioned by Ducange, Fabricius, and Mullach. After Conring having proved to be right about a Cologne edition dated 1574, I am more inclined to think it possible that he may be again correct as to an edition printed at Rome in 1570, but no copy is as yet forthcoming. As to a 1572 Padua edition, denied by Beckmann and by Dr. Kopp, it is quite as likely (as I have already said*) that there were editions issued there in 1572, 1573, as that there were, for certain, Cologne issues of 1572, 1573, 1574. I am not without hope that I may at some time or other be able to communicate to the Society an account of one, if not both of these editions. It would not be less improbable than this present account of the 1574 edition, of which I was myself most doubtful six years ago, and of the most rare Padua edition, of which I had no expectation of ever coming across a copy.

13. The result at present is that of the nine editions of Democritus quoted from all known authorities in my former paper, descriptions of six of them from actual copies have now been laid before the Society. Three still remain doubtful—Rome, 1570; Padua, 1572; Nürnberg (in German), 1717.

POSTSCRIPT. *November* 28, 1890.

Since the preceding was read to the Society, I have been enabled, by the kindness of the librarian, to examine the Cambridge University Library copy of the Padua edition, and find it far more interesting than I could have supposed, so much so that I have had a photo-facsimile made of the title-page to render my remarks

---

* *Proceedings of the Philosophical Society of Glasgow,* 1885, vol. xvi., p. 42, § 10.

intelligible.   Two things will be noticed: 1st, the misprint Ibderita, corrected to Abderita, by printing a larger A over the I, but obliquely so as to obliterate it as much as possible ; and 2nd, the position of the middle I in the date.   It looks as if the date had been originally MDLXXII, and that another I had been stuck in afterwards.   This seems to me to be conclusive.   The work really appeared at Padua in 1572, and then it was re-dated and issued in 1573.   It is impossible, of course, to say whether all the copies were re-dated, but the only two that I know of at present seem to have been dealt with in the same way.   It *is* possible, however, that some escaped, so that there is a chance that such a copy may be met with, but the present copy, from the way the date has been altered, seems to me to leave no doubt that the book was issued originally in 1572.

This simplifies the entire subject, and I am gratified that the inspection of the book has confirmed my anticipations.

I must reserve for a subsequent paper a fuller account of this edition, and a comparison of it with that of Cologne, 1572.

APPENDIX.   *February* 25, 1891.

In my original paper I described the British Museum copy of the Cologne 1573 edition of Mizaldus' *Memorabilia,* but with less detail than that of 1572.   I now give a fuller account of the 1573 edition, for comparison with that of 1574.   After minute examination of the 1573 and 1574 issues, I can detect no difference except in the date and in the dislocation of signature B2 (whereby the 2 has got separated from the B) in the 1574 edition.*   So far as I can see, the 1574 edition is simply a re-issue of surplus copies of the 1573 edition with altered date, for slips that would have been corrected in an entirely new edition are left unaltered : thus, signature S5 wants the 5 in both issues ; folio 228, line 1, the I in PHI... is similarly defective in both, and in many similar minute points they agree.

---

* This dislocation, I find, is only in the Cambridge University Library copy.   The Aberdeen copy, which I have since examined, is quite regular.

DEMOCRITVS ABDERITA DE ARTE MAGNA,

Siue de rebus naturalibus.

Nec non Synesii, & Pelagii, & Stephani Alexandrini, & Michaelis Pselli in eundem commentaria.

Dominico Pizimentio Vibonensi Interprete.

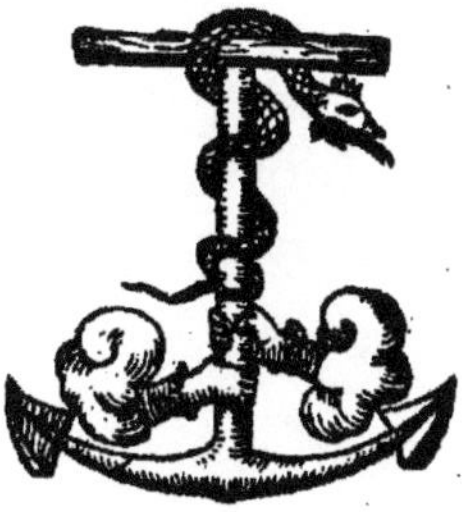

PATAVII
Apud Simonem Galignanum
MDLXXIII.

Maclure Macdonald & Co

ANTONII MIZALDI MON-
luciani Galli, Medici,

MEMORABI-
LIVM, SIVE ARCA-
NORVM OMNIS GE-
NERIS,
PER APHORISMOS DI-
geſtorum, Centuriæ IX.

ET

DEMOCRITVS ABDERITA, DE
rebus Naturalibus, & Myſticis.

Cum

Synesii, et Pelagii
Commentarijs.

Interprete de Græca lingua,
Dominico Pizimentio Vibonen-
ſi Italo.
Præfatio,
In omnes hoſce libros.

COLONIAE.
Apud Ioannem Birckmannum
. Anno D.M.LXXIII.

Cum Gratia & Priuilegio Cæſar. Maieſtat.

24°. *Sigs. in 12.* *Title; *2r to ***7v [or 30 leaves], Præfatio *to Thomas Redinger, dated:* Calendis | Martijs. M.D. | LXXII. Vbio | rum Colo- | nia (·.·); ***8r to ****9r [or 14 leaves], Index Rervm | præcipuarum; **** 10, 11, 12, *are wanting in the Museum Copy. The title and preliminary matter, therefore, occupy 48 ff. [3 blanks wanting] not numbered. The text is foliated consecutively from* f[1] *to* f. 245, *or sigs.* A to X6 *in 12's. Text stops on* X5 *verso,* X6 *is blank. Sig.* B. *runs quite uniformly, and* B2 *is not dislocated. Collation:* f. 1, *Title, v. blank.*

*2 recto: De Mizaldi | Arcanis, Nec Non | Graecis In Demo- | critvm, Caeteris- | que Chemiæ scripto- | ribus, | Præfatio. | Ad Clarissimvm No- | bilitate, doctrina, prudentiaqúe virum, | Thomam Redingervm | Silesivm. |

This preface ends on ***7 v. (= *f. 31 v.) with the words: comparatur. Vale.* Calendis | Martijs. M.D. | LXXII. Vbio | rum Colo- | nia (·.·). *With no scroll ornament. On* f. *32 r. begins Index Rerum which ends on* f. *45 r. Verso is blank, and the three blank leaves to complete* *the signature are wanting. The introductory matter is not numbered. The text of Mizaldus' treatise then begins on leaf* A1, f. [1], *and goes down to the recto of f. 212. Verso is blank.*

F. 213 r. contains the title to the Chemical Tracts, as follows :—

Ex | Venerandæ Græcæ vetustatis de ar- | te Chymica, relliquijs. | Democritvs | Abderyta, De Arte | Sacra: Sive, De Rebvs | naturalibus & my- | sticis, | Necnon | Synesij, & Pelagij, Antiquorum | Philosophorum : in eundem, | Commentaria. | Interprete | Dominico Pizimentio Vibo- | nensi Italo. | *Small scroll ornament, as in 1572.*

F. 213 verso is blank.

F. 214 recto contains Pizimenti's preface : Ad‡Amplissi- | mvm Illvstris- | simvmqve Seqva- | num, | *which ends f. 218 recto, with the words :* Stephani Alexandrini, Olympiodori, | & Pelagij cōmentaria, in eundem | Democritum propediem ex | pecta. Datum Romæ. | Calend. Septemb. | M.D.LXX. | (· . ·) | *The catchword is* Ex. *Then*

F. 218 verso begins : Ex Rebvs Na- | tvralibus Et My- | sticis Demo- | criti. | (· . ·) | Natvra naturâ | gaudet : &c., *which ends f. 227 verso :* omisi cùm liberè in alijs etiam | meis scriptis pertracta- | rim. In hoc scripto | valete. | (· . ·) |

F. 228 recto : Synesii Phi | losophi Ad Dio- | scorvm. In Librvm | Democriti. | Scholia, | (· . ·) | *followed by the same scroll ornament as in 1574. This ends f. 238 verso.*

F. 239 recto : Pelagii Philo- | sophi De Eadem | Divina Et Sacra | arte. | (· . ·) *ends f. 245 verso, followed by a similar scroll ornament to that on f. 228.*

A blank leaf ends the volume.

Philosophical Society of Glasgow.

1891-92.

JOHN FERGUSON,

M.A., LL.D., F.S.A., F.S.A.Scot., F.C.S.,

ON THE

FIRST EDITION OF THE CHEMICAL WRITINGS OF

DEMOCRITUS AND SYNESIUS.

PART III.

GÖTTINGEN TITLE-PAGE.

DEMOCRITVS
ABDERITA
DE ARTE
MAGNA,

Siue de rebus naturalibus.

Necnon Synesii, & Pelagii, & Stephani Alexandrini, & Michaelis Pselli in eundem commentaria.

Dominico Pizimentio Vibonensi Interprete.

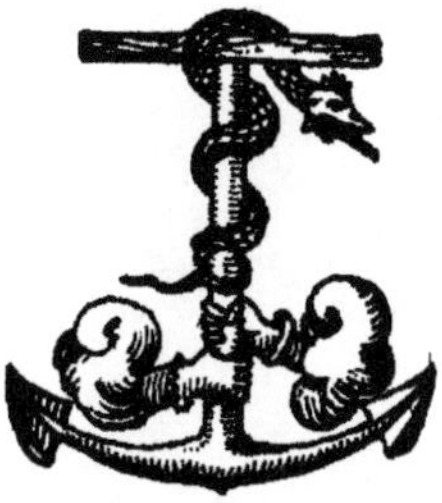

PATAVII
Apud Simonem Galignanum
M D LXXIII.

MACLURE, MACDONALD & CO.

[FROM THE *PROCEEDINGS* OF THE PHILOSOPHICAL SOCIETY OF GLASGOW.]

On the First Edition of the Chemical Writings of Democritus and Synesius. Part III. By Professor JOHN FERGUSON, M.A., LL.D., F.S.A., F.S.A.Scot., F.C.S.

[Read before the Society, 18th November, 1891.]

(PLATE III.)

1. At the corresponding meeting last Session, 19th Nov., 1890, I communicated to the Society an account of a very rare copy in the University Library, Cambridge, of the Latin translation, by Pizimenti, of the chemical writings of Democritus and certain other Greek authors, printed at Padua in 1573. To the paper, since printed,[1] I have added a facsimile of the title page, and have pointed out that, from the unsymmetrical position of the middle I in the date, the date must have been altered from MDLXXII. to MDLXXIII. by the insertion of an additional I, subsequent to the original printing. I also drew the inference that, unless all the copies had been similarly altered, one might still be found bearing the date 1572.

2. On subsequent consideration it occurred to me that, if the date had been altered by the insertion of an extra I, it was improbable that the unsymmetricalness of its position would be the same in every copy, and I could not help observing that in the only other copy of the book I then knew, that at Göttingen, neither Beckmann nor Kopp had taken notice of such an obvious feature of the title page.

3. To confirm my view of the matter I wrote, so long ago as last February, to Professor Dziatzko, principal librarian at Göttingen, with a photograph of the title page of the Cambridge copy, and in reply to certain questions which I asked received a most courteous

---

[1] *Proceedings* of the Philosophical Society of Glasgow, 1891, vol. XXII., p. 301, Postscript.

reply,[2] giving me complete information on the points required.
The following is a translation of the parts in question :—

> " 1st. The two title pages agree exactly, except in the figure I in
> the date.

> " 2ndly. Under the initial A of ABDERITA (larger and placed
> somewhat obliquely) stands also in our copy an I, which had been
> scraped out before the A was printed over it.

> " 3rd. The three ones in our copy stand thus [with a sketch of their
> arrangement]. Obviously the centre type was not in the printing, but
> was afterwards inserted in the space between the other two by hand,
> which would come out differently in the different copies. The inserted
> I seems to be *a shade* smaller, the other figures are equal."

4. It is plain from this that in the Göttingen copy the centre I
occupies a different position relatively to the other two from what
it does in the Cambridge copy. Of course, if the date had been
originally printed MDLXXIII., it would have been the same in
every copy. This was exactly the point that I was desirous of
settling. Comparison of the two title pages shows that the middle
I was inserted subsequent to the printing of the title page, and
Professor Dziatzko, from what he says, has obviously arrived
independently at the same conclusion. But just because in the
Göttingen copy the symmetry happens to be fairly complete, the
alteration of the date has escaped the notice both of Beckmann
and Kopp, and one may question whether, without another copy
for comparison, the alteration could have been easily detected
in the Göttingen copy alone. To complete this part of the subject,
I now intend to get, if possible, a photograph of the Göttingen
copy, which will exhibit more distinctly than any amount of
description the difference between it and the Cambridge copy.[3]

5. I have had recently other opportunities for investigating
this question.

During a visit which I paid this last September to the Bibliothèque Nationale at Paris, I was gratified at finding another copy

---

[2] Dated: Königl. Universitäts-Bibliothek, Göttingen, Feb. 7, 1891.

[3] February, 1892. I have since got a photograph of the title page of the
Göttingen copy, through the kindness of the authorities of the University
Library there, from which a lithographic copy has been made. It requires
no comment, and all that has to be done is to compare it with the facsimiles
of the copies in Cambridge University Library and the Bibliothèque
Nationale to see that the date is differently arranged. Though this facsimile is rather smaller than the original and the other two facsimiles,
that does not affect the main point under discussion.

[redacted]

DEMOCRITVS

AB DERITA
DE ARTE
MAGNA.

Siue de rebus naturalibus.

Nec non Synesii, & Pelagii, & Stephani Alexandrini, & Michaelis Pselli in eundem commentaria.

Dominico Pizimentio Viboneñsi
Interprete.

P A T A V I I
Apud Simonem Galignanum
M D LXXII.

of this book, dated 1573, the title page of which I was very kindly allowed to have photographed for me by M. Dujardin, the well-known photo-engraver. From this a zincograph has been made by Messrs. Walker & Boutall, of Clifford's Inn, London, which enables the difference between it and the Cambridge copy to be displayed.

One difference is that the initial A in ABDERITA is considerably larger than that in the Cambridge copy, although, like it (and the Göttingen copy), it is placed obliquely so as to hide the I.

As for the date, the Paris copy also has the middle I misplaced, so that it resembles the Cambridge copy very closely : but careful examination shows—1st, an almost imperceptible difference in the spacing ; and, 2nd, that the middle I is not of exactly the same length in the two copies.

By these facts the view is much corroborated that the original date was MDLXXII., but that it was altered to MDLXXIII. by hand, so that different copies exhibit different positions of the middle figure.

6. Since that visit my attention has been directed to the Catalogue[4] of the Library in the Barberini Palace at Rome, in which there are apparently two copies of the book, dated 1573. I have not as yet been able to obtain any description of these copies, but I hope not only to be able to lay an account of them before the Society, but to include photographs of the title-pages as well, so as to complete the series as far as I can.

7. There are thus five (?) copies of the book, three of which *certainly* (and I think it is reasonable to suppose that the other two as well) bear evidence of the fact that the date 1573 is an amended or altered one from 1572.

When, therefore, I argued seven years ago,[5] from the fact of my having found a copy of the Cologne edition of 1572, that there must be an Italian edition earlier than that, or at least as early, I was induced to do so from the improbability of a translation by an Italian being first published at Cologne, and that not as an independent work, but as a mere appendix to the quite different

---

[4] Index, 1681.

[5] *Proceedings* of the Philosophical Society of Glasgow, 1885, vol. XVI., p. 41, § 10.

work of Mizaldus, which had been published at Paris six years earlier. I had not had at that time the opportunity of comparing the Padua edition with that of Cologne, else I could have spoken with more certainty, and I did not anticipate that the Padua edition of 1573 would be itself one of the strongest pieces of evidence in support of the view I advanced.

8. A visit, however, to the Bibliothèque Ste. Geneviève at Paris set finally the whole question at rest, for there, at last, was forthcoming a copy of the Padua edition, dated 1572, and it was satisfactory to find that the possibility which I had suggested at the close of last year's paper,[6] of some copies having escaped alteration, had become a certainty by the discovery of one of them. Of the title page of this edition also I hope to have a photograph, so that it may be printed along with the present paper.[7]

9. At the conclusion of the first paper on this subject, I gave a list of nine editions, of which I had seen four, knew of one on reliable authority, and was very doubtful about the remaining four. The list as it now stands revised contains seven editions, all of which I have seen; the remaining two are still very doubtful. The lists are as follow :—

1884 List.

		Authorities.
1570 (?)...	Rome, (?)	Conring.
1572 ...	Cologne, ...	Ferguson.
1572 (?)...	Padua, (?)	Ducange.
1573 ...	Cologne (previously unknown),	Ferguson.
1573 ...	Padua, ...	Beckmann, Kopp.
1574 (?)...	Cologne, (?)	Reinesius, Conring.
1717 ...	Nürnberg (in Latin), ...	Ferguson.
1717 (?)...	Nürnberg (in German), (?) ...	Dufresnoy, Schmieder.
1869 ...	Braunschweig, ...	Dr. Kopp's reprint.

1891 List.

1. Padua, 1572,	... Bibliothèque Ste. Geneviève, Paris.
2. Cologne, 1572,	... Hunterian Library, ⎫ Glasgow.
3. ,, ,,	... University Library, ⎭
4. ,, ,,	... University Library, Cambridge.
5. ,, ,,	... New College, Oxford.
6. ,, ,,	... Trinity College, Cambridge.
7. ,, ,,	... Copy seen by Dr. Kopp.

[6] See above, § 1, Note [1].

[7] June 1, 1892.—I have not succeeded as yet in getting this photograph.

8.	Padua, 1573, ...	...	University Library, Cambridge.
9.	,, ,, ...	...	Bibliothèque Nationale.
10.	,, ,, ...	...	University Library, Göttingen.
11, 12.	,, ,, ...	...	Barberini Library, Rome.
13.	Cologne, 1573,	...	British Museum.
14.	Cologne, 1574,	...	University Library, Cambridge.
15.	,, ,,	...	University Library, Aberdeen.
16.	Nürnberg, 1717,	...	Young Collection, Glasgow.
17.	Braunschweig, 1869,..		Reprint in Kopp's *Beiträge.*

I have still to see the edition of Rome, 1570, and of Nürnberg, 1717, in German.

10. No previous writer on the subject has seen more than one, or at most two of these editions which I have now described, and many of those who have mentioned the book at all have done so in an unsatisfactory manner, because they had seen no copies and took their descriptions from other writers.

The two chief authorities, for example, for the 1573 Padua edition, from personal examination, Beckmann and Dr. Kopp, denied the existence of an earlier dated edition, and went the length of marking as erroneous the statements of other writers who spoke of editions previous to that one.

The authorities for the different editions may be now briefly enumerated :—

The 1572 Padua edition is mentioned by Fabricius,[8] doubtfully by Ducange,[9] without any question by Mullach,[10] and descriptively by Gmelin.[11] Beckmann[12] says that Fabricius cannot have

---

[8] *Bibliotheca Græca*, Hamburgi, 1708, I., p. 809.

[9] "Editus dicitur Patavii anno 1572. nescio an & Græcè." Index Auctorum Græcorum, col. 25, at the end of the second volume of the *Glossarium ad Scriptores Mediæ & Infimæ Græcitatis.* Lugduni, 1688, folio. In my former reference to Ducange's statement (*Proceedings*, Phil. Soc., Glasgow, 1885, vol. XVI., p. 42, § 10), I said that he could not tell whether it was in Greek or in Latin, and I was led to do so by Kopp's (*Beiträge zur Geschichte der Chemie*, Braunschweig, 1869, p. 113, Note 22) reading : "nescio an græce." Ducange's own reading, however, is different, and means that he was not sure if the Greek was published as well as the Latin.

[10] *Democriti Abderitae Operum Fragmenta*, Berolini, 1843, p. 157 (compare p. 158). Mullach simply copies from Fabricius (*Bibl. Græca*, 1708, I., p. 809) without acknowledgment.

[11] *Geschichte der Chemie*, Göttingen, 1797, I., p. 21.

[12] *Beyträge zur Geschichte der Erfindungen*, Leipzig, 1792, III., p. 376, Note 29.

seen the book, as he does not give either the title or date correctly. The date is certainly correct; and as for the title, Fabricius, I think, was giving a description of the contents of the book, rather than the actual words of the title. Dr. Kopp agrees tacitly with this criticism of Beckmann's, which, all the same, is wrong.

The 1572 Cologne reprint is mentioned by Mercklin,[13] Fabricius,[14] by Lambeck[15] in his commentaries, and by Fuchs.[16] Kopp, who was in doubt about it in 1869, informed me afterwards that he had seen a copy.

The 1573 Padua edition is given by Fabricius,[17] by Reinesius,[18] in the *Beytrag*,[19] by Beckmann[20] (who has printed a careful account of it from the Göttingen copy), by Fuchs,[21] by S. F. G. Hoffmann,[22] Dufresnoy,[23] Brunet,[24] and Graesse,[25] by Hoefer,[26] by Reuvens,[27] by Sprengel,[28] by J. F. Gmelin,[29] by Schmieder,[30] by Kopp, and by Berthelot.[31]

---

[13] *Lindenius Renovatus*, Norimbergæ, 1686, p. 243.

[14] *Bibliotheca Græca*, Hamburgi, 1724, XII., p. 709.

[15] *Commentariorum . . . Liber Sextus*, Vindob., 1780, p. 383, quoted by Kopp, *Beyträge*, 1869, p. 111, note 13.

[16] *Repertorium der Chemischen Litteratur*, Jena u. Leipzig, 1806, p. 2.

[17] *Bibliotheca Græca*, Hamburgi, 1717, VIII., p. 232, Note [1]. *Ibid.* 1724, XII., p. 709. Although Fabricius mentions this and the Cologne 1572 reprint together on p. 709, the discrepancy of date and difference of contents do not seem to have impressed him, from which I infer that he had not compared, or had not been able to compare, the two editions.

[18] Fabricius, *Bibliotheca Græca*, Hamburgi, 1724, XII., p. 750.

[19] *Beytrag zur Geschichte der höhern Chemie*, Leipzig, 1785, p. 578.

[20] *Beyträge zur Geschichte der Erfindungen*, Leipzig, 1792, III., p. 376, Note 29.

[21] *Repertorium der Chemischen Litteratur*, Jena u. Leipzig, 1806, p. 2.

[22] *Lexicon Bibliographicum*, Lipsiae, 1833, 8°, II., p. 9.

[23] *Histoire de la Philosophie Hermetique*, Paris, 1742, III., p. 146. This is under Democritus; but under Synesius (*Ibid.* p. 306) he quotes the 1572 edition.

[24] *Manuel du Libraire*, Paris, 1861, II., 584.

[25] *Trésor de Livres Rares et Précieux*, Dresde, 1861, II., 356.

[26] *Histoire de la Chimie*, 1842, I., p. 266, and 1866, I., p. 277.

[27] *Lettres à M. Letronne*, Leide, 1830, 4°, Troisième Lettre, p. 70, Note (c).

[28] *Histoire de la Médicine*, Paris, 1815, II., p. 158.

[29] *Geschichte der Chemie*, Göttingen, 1797, I., p. 314, Note *m*.

[30] *Geschichte der Alchemie*, Halle, 1832, p. 64.

[31] *Les Origines de l'Alchimie*, Paris, 1885, p. 105, &c., and *Collection des Anciens Alchimistes Grecs*, Paris, 1888, III. (Traduction), p. 378.

The 1573 Cologne edition is mentioned by no writer, except myself, and the first notice appeared in the *Proceedings* of this Society.[32]

The 1574 Cologne edition is mentioned by Borellius,[33] Mercklin,[34] and Reinesius,[35] and they are followed by a number of modern writers, Dufresnoy,[36] Fuchs,[37] Hoffmann,[38] Gmelin,[39] Schmieder,[40] and Graesse.[41] Conring[42] also quotes, incidentally, an edition of this date.

The Nürnberg edition, in Latin, is mentioned by Hoffmann,[43] Brunet,[44] and Graesse.[45]

The Brunswick reprint of 1869 is contained in Dr. Kopp's *Beiträge*, and is accessible to everyone.

It is singular that Borrichius, so far as I have observed, makes no reference to any of the editions of Pizimenti's translation, although he himself devoted so much attention to the Greek alchemists. Morhof,[46] on the other hand, though he mentions Pizimenti's translation, and speaks both of the Padua edition and that annexed to Mizaldus, gives no date for either. Apparently he had no copy at hand.

11. The two editions still wanting are—first, that of Rome, 1570, mentioned by Conring,[47] who probably founded his statement on the date of the dedication. I think it hardly probable

---

[32] *Proceedings* of the Philosophical Society of Glasgow, 1885, vol. XVI., p. 40, §9.

[33] *Bibliotheca Chimica*, Paris, 1654, p. 75; Heidelbergæ, 1656, p. 71.

[34] *Lindenius Renovatus*, Norimbergæ, 1686, p. 243.

[35] Fabricius, *Bibliotheca Græca*, Hamburgi, 1724, XII., p. 749.

[36] *Histoire de la Philosophie Hermetique*, Paris, 1742, III., p. 147, 306.

[37] *Repertorium der Chemischen Litteratur*, Jena u. Leipzig, 1806, p. 2.

[38] *Lexicon Bibliographicum*, Lipsiae, 1833, II., p. 9.

[39] *Geschichte der Chemie*, Göttingen, 1797, I., p. 314, Note o. Gmelin, however, mentions it in connection with Pelagius.

[40] *Geschichte der Alchemie*, Halle, 1832, p. 64.

[41] *Trésor de Livres Rares et Précieux*, 1861, Dresde, II., p. 356.

[42] *De Hermetica Medicina*, Helmestadii, 1648, p. 27; 1669, p. 29.

[43] *Lexicon Bibliographicum*, Lipsiae, 1833, p. 9.

[44] *Manuel du Libraire*, Paris, 1861, II., p. 584.

[45] *Trésor de Livres Rares et Précieux*, 1861, Dresde, II., p. 356.

[46] *Polyhistor*, Lubecæ, 1714, tom. II., lib. II., pars I., cap. VII., §6; tom. I., lib. I., cap. XI., §34. See also tom. II., lib. I., cap. V., §1, where he speaks of Venice as the place of printing; "Si rectè memini," he adds. But Padua was the place.

[47] *De Hermetica Medicina*, Helmestadii, 1648, p. 27; 1669, p. 29

that there is an edition of that date. ˙ The circumstances mentioned below as to the printing of the 1572 edition at Padua seem to me adverse to such an edition. The other edition is that in German, Nürnberg, 1717. It is mentioned by Dufresnoy,[48] and by Schmieder.[49] I am entirely doubtful about this edition. It is possible that a Latin and German translation should be published in the same year, or even simultaneously in the same year, at the same place, and by the same or by different people; but while I have seen the Latin edition,[50] I have not seen the German, or any account of it, except by Dufresnoy and Schmieder, who do not always excel in accuracy, and who on this occasion have possibly been misled, as I said before.[51] At the same time, I should myself quite miss the full benefit of the bibliographic lesson that this whole subject conveys, if I were to be so rash as to assert that a 1570 edition of Rome, or a 1717 German translation, either did not or could not exist. I have given some reasons for strongly doubting their existence, but a copy of either may turn up any day, and stultify all hypotheses, however plausible.

12. As far, however, as a 1717 German translation is concerned, I think the following facts settle its non-existence :—

1°. A German translation of the chemical writings of the Abbot Synesius by Roth-Scholtz was published at Nürnberg in 1718, by the heirs of Joh. Dan. Tauber, along with the works (also in German) of Sendivogius. On the last page of Synesius' tract there is a small list of works to be had from the same publishers, and in that list is Democritus' *De Rebus Sacris*, in *Latin.*

2°. In 1720 (first edition 1718) Roth-Scholtz published an edition in Latin of the chemical works of Rivinus and of Vigani, at Nürnberg, by Tauber's heirs. In separate lists of Tauber's books contained in this edition the *German* version of Synesius is mentioned twice, but of Democritus' *De Rebus Sacris* only the *Latin* edition is advertised.

3°. In 1727 (second edition 1735) Tauber's heirs at Nürnberg published Roth-Scholtz's *Bibliotheca Chemica, oder Catalogus von Chymischen*

---

[48] *Histoire de la Philosophie Hermetique*, Paris, 1742, III., p. 147.

[49] *Geschichte der Alchemie*, Halle, 1832, p. 65.

[50] *Proceedings* of the Philosophical Society of Glasgow, 1885, vol. XVI., p. 43, §13.

[51] *Proceedings* of the Philosophical Society of Glasgow, 1885, vol. XVI., p. 43, §13, p. 45, §16.

Büchern. On p. 54 appears : Democritus abderyta græcus de Rebus sacris . . . Norimbergæ, 1717 ; the Latin edition formerly described by me,[52] but not a single syllable about a German version.

If there had been a German translation of Democritus in 1717, published by Tauber's heirs, it would surely have been mentioned in some one of his advertisements, like the Latin edition. It might, of course, have been printed at Nürnberg by some other firm, but there is not a tittle of evidence in support of such a perfectly gratuitous assumption. Until, therefore, a copy of a German translation, published at Nürnberg in 1717, either by Tauber's heirs or some one else, has been actually seen, described, and the place where it exists specified, I must refuse to accept the statements of Dufresnoy and Schmieder.

13. Although this investigation has been confined entirely to the Latin translation of the Greek alchemical authors, it would be an unpardonable omission if no notice were taken of the most important contribution that has been recently made to the subject by the publication of the original Greek text itself. This is contained in the edition of the Greek Alchemists, printed from the finest of all the manuscripts,[53] that preserved in St. Mark's Library at Venice, edited by M. Berthelot, and published in Paris in 1888, in 3 vols., 4°. From this one can now see with what accuracy and completeness Pizimenti did the work of translation from the MS. which came to his hands by a Greek from Corfu; that, however, belongs to a different department of the subject, into which I do not intend at present to enter, as I may have an opportunity of doing so elsewhere.

14. I may now, however, give a detailed view of the contents of Pizimenti's translation :—

a 1, the title.

a 2 *r* to a 5 *r*, numbered fol. 2 *r* to f. 5 *r*, Pizimenti's address or preface to Cardinal Antonius Perrenottus. It ends : Datum Romæ. Calend. Septemb. M.D.LXX.[54]

---

[52] *Proceedings* of the Philosophical Society of Glasgow, 1885, vol. XVI., p. 43, § 13.

[53] For a list of these MSS., thirty in all, reference may be made to my address on the subject when President of the Chemical Section of this Society in 1876. See *Proceedings*, X., p. 373.

[54] Though addressed to different persons, this preface is the same in the Padua, 1572, 1573, and Cologne, 1572, 1573, 1574 editions, with certain

Sig. a 5 *v*, or f. 5 *v* : Ex Rebvs Natvra- | libvs, Et Mysticis | Democriti. | Ends b 3 (misprinted 5) *r*, or f. 11 *r*.

Sig. b 3 *v*, or f. 11 *v* : Dioscoro Sacer- | doti Magni Serapí- | dis in Alexandria | Deo Favente. | Synesivs Philosophvs | S.P.D. | Ends c 2 *r*, or f. 18 *r*.

Sig. c 2 *v*, or f. 18 *v* : Pelagii Philosophi | De Eadem Magna | Arte. | Ends c 7 *r*, or f. 23 *r*.

What follows is not contained in the Cologne reprints.

Sig. c 7 *r*, or f. 23 *r* : Stephani Alexandrini | Oecumenici Philosophi, & Magistri | Magnę huius Artis Auri confi- | ciendi, Actio prima. | Dominico Pizimentio | Interprete. |

Sig. d 1 *v*, f. 25 *v*, Actio secunda.

Sig. d 6 *r*, f. 30 *r* : Eivsdem Stephani Epistola | ad Theodorum. |

Sig. d 7 *r*, f. 31 *r* : Eivsdem Stephani De Ma- | teriali Mundo Deo fauente, | Actio tertia. |

Sig. e 2 *r*, f. 34 *r* : Eivsdem Stephani In Id, Qvod | ad operationem facit, diuina bene | ficentia, Actio quarta. |

Sig. e 7 *r*, f. 39 *r* : Eivsdem Stephani In Hvivs | artis opus Deo fauente. | Actio quinta. |

Sig. f 2 *r*, f. 42 *r* : Eivsdem Stephani Deo | fauente, Actio sexta. |

Sig. f 8 *r*, f. 48 *r* : Eivsdem Stephani Philosophi | Deo fauente, Actio septima. |

Sig. g 5 *v*, f. 53 *v* (misnumbered f. 29) : Eiusdem Stephani œcumenici philosophi | actio octaua de huius artis sectione. |

Sig h 1 *r*, f. 57 *r* : Eiusdem Stephani philosophi ad Heraclium | Regem, ope diuina, actio nona. |

Sig. i 1 *r*, f. 65 *r* : Michaelis Pselli Epistola | ad Xiphilinum Patri- archam. De Auri | conficiendi ratione, | Dominico Pizimentio] Vibonensi Interprete. |

Ends i 6 *v*, f. 70 *v*, and after the text comes the licence in Italian.

15. Pizimenti's translation is dedicated by himself to Cardinal Antonius Perrenottus, and is dated Rome, Sept. 1, 1570. He concludes in saying that, if this work is agreeable, the Cardinal

---

exceptions, detailed in §§ 15, 17. I have noted also the following various readings :—

PATAV., 1572, 1573.	COLON., 1572, 1573, 1574.
f. 2 *r*, line 14, 15, longè, la- | req́;	f. 214 *r*, line 16, longè lateq́;
f. 2 *r*, line 18, 19, referun- | tur	{ f. 214 *r*, line 21, referuntur : 1572. { f. 214 *r*, line 21, referuatur ; 1573, 1574.
f. 5 *r*, line 7, ὁμοτροφον ἀπολλωνος	f. 217 *v*, line 28-9, omotrophon A- | pollonos
f. 5 *r*, line 10, δοτορ εαΟν Græcè	{ f. 218 *r*, line 4, dotor eaon Grę- | cè, 1572. { f. 218 *r*, line 4, dotor eaŏ Græ- | cè, 1573, 1574.

may hope soon for a translation of the Commentaries on Democritus of Olympiodorus and others.[55] Olympiodorus and the others would, in fact, be contained in the original MS. he had, of which, however, he published only the authors above mentioned. Apparently Pizimenti never carried his translations any further, for Leo Allatius, who, at a much later date, 1661 or thereabouts (Kopp, *Beiträge*, p. 248, 249), meditated an edition of the Greek alchemists in the Vatican Library, gave a list of those he meant to publish, and enumerated those of which a translation had been made by Pizimenti. The list comprises only those mentioned above, so that Leo Allatius knew of no more.

16. But even from Pizimenti's own translation one work seems to have been omitted from the printed edition.

The work as it stands concludes with the licence. It is in Italian, and runs as follows :—

> Io fra Massimiano da Crema, ho ueduto il | presente libro di carte 83. nel quale sono De- | mocrito, Synesio, & Pelagio stampati, & Stef- | fano Alessandrino con Michele Psello, & O- | stane scritti à penna, & non ho trovato, che | repugni alla fede Catholica. |
>
> Idem qui supra Fr. Maximianus | Inq. Paduæ. |

> I, Frater Maximianus da Crema, have seen the present book of 83 leaves, in which are Democritus, Synesius, and Pelagius, printed, and Stephanus Alexandrinus with Michael Psellus and Ostanes in manuscript (or written by pen), and have not seen anything therein opposed to the Catholic faith.
>
> (Signed) Fra. Maximianus, Inq. Paduæ.

From the printed edition Ostanes has been omitted. This licence seems to me to be very curious, and to throw some light on the history of the book, though most unfortunately it has no date. But it is certainly remarkable that when the licence was drawn out the officer, or inspector, or *inquisitor*, had submitted to him a book partly in print, partly in MS.

The printed portion—assuming that it is the Padua edition he saw, and not a Roman one of 1570 or thereby—containing Democritus, Synesius, and Pelagius, occupies the leaves 5 verso to 23 recto; the MS. portion occupies, after printing, leaves 23

---

[55] Vale, & si hæc tibi non ingrata | fuisse significaueris, quæ, ut Hieronymo Fagiolo | uiro humanissimo, ac mecum summa familiarita- | te coniunctissimo petenti gratificarer, latina face | re uolui Olympiodori & aliorum commentaria in | eundem Democritum propediem expecta. | Datum Romæ. Calend. Septemb. M.D.LXX. |

recto to 70 verso, and contains only Stephanus and Psellus, Ostanes not having been printed. The last two leaves of the sheet are blank.

17. On comparing the Padua edition of 1573 with Birckmann's Cologne edition, either of 1572, 1573, or 1574 (for in this respect they are all alike), there are three things that are specially noteworthy :—

1°. Birckmann's edition contains Democritus, Synesius, and Pelagius, *only*, not Stephanus and Psellus.

2°. Pizimenti's preface or dedication is addressed, not to Perrenottus, but to Joannes Metellus Sequanus.

3°. This dedication is identical with that in the Padua edition, even to the date, Rome, Sept. 1, 1570, except at the very close. Instead of Pizimenti promising to send Olympiodorus and the others, he is made to say that the dedicatee may soon look for the commentaries of Stephanus Alexandrinus, Olympiodorus, and Pelagius.

Pelagius is, I suspect, a misprint for *Psellus*, because Pelagius was already printed.

It is plain from this that Birckmann had no copy of Stephanus Alexandrinus, which is contained in the Padua edition.

Birckmann, or whoever it was who wrote the preface to the 1572 edition of Mizaldus, says that, when he was half through the printing of Mizaldus, Sequanus sent him the Latin translation of Democritus, Synesius, and Pelagius, which, in compliance with Sequanus' advice, and as intrinsically appropriate, he had added on to the edition. This must have been prior to March 1st, 1572, the date of the preface.

Apparently, therefore, in reprinting Pizimenti's dedication, Sequanus' name was coolly substituted for Perrenottus' (which misled me formerly,[56] before I had seen the Padua edition), and the end of the dedication[57] was also altered so as to conceal the absence of Stephanus Alexandrinus and Psellus, and make appear as if they were coming shortly. Either, however, Sequanus never

---

[56] *Proceedings*, 1885, vol. XVI., p. 42, § 10.

[57] The dedication concludes thus in Birckmann's edition (1572, f. 218) :— " Vale, & si hæc tibi non ingrata fuisse significaueris, quæ, vt Hieronymo Fagiolo viro humanissimo : ac mecum summa familiaritate coniunctissimo, petenti, gratificarer, latina facere volui : Stephani Alexandrini, Olympiodori, & Pelagii cōmentaria, in eundem Democritum propediem expecta. Datum, Romę. Calend. Septemb. M.D.LXX." This should be compared with the conclusion in the Padua edition, as given in § 15, Note [55].

sent the finished printed edition of 1572, or else Birckmann was unable or did not think it worth while to reprint Stephanus and the rest.

18. The question, therefore, arises, what was the *copy* from which Birckmann printed? was it manuscript, or was it the printed Padua edition? If the former, Sequanus must have got a copy somehow from Pizimenti, and, in that case, one should hardly expect Pizimenti to give him a copy of the dedication to Perrenottus with permission to have it dedicated to himself.

It is, however, a remarkable coincidence that the portion printed by Birckmann should not only tally with the first 23 leaves of the Padua edition, but that this should be exactly the portion which was in print when Maximianus penned his licence.

It is plausible, therefore, to infer that Sequanus got possession of this printed portion, dedication and all, and sent it on to Birckmann, either himself making the alterations in the dedication to suit the circumstances, or getting or leaving Birckmann to make them.

In this latter case this portion at least of the Padua edition must have been printed before March 1st, 1572, the date of Birckmann's preface. Here it seems to me is additional evidence from the very facts that at first sight seemed to contradict it, and which originated this whole investigation, that there must have been an edition of a book by an Italian in Italy before one which appeared at Cologne as a mere addendum, and an accidental one, too, to another book. Even before I saw the copy dated 1572, I was convinced, by a comparison of the Cambridge copy with Birckmann's 1572 edition, that the former, though apparently dated 1573, was in reality the earlier. I am now more strongly persuaded of that fact than ever.

19. There still remains another and more difficult problem, of which at present I can offer no solution satisfactory to myself, that is —Why was the date altered from 1572 to 1573 in the Padua edition? One explanation that occurred to me was that the book had been printed: title page, with the date 1572; dedication and text as far as f. 23, *i.e.*, to the end of Pelagius (which is practically the first three sheets, viz., a, b, and c), but was stopped at that point on account of some difficulty or informality about the licence, or possibly that it was printing without a licence at all. This would explain the peculiar and

minute specification in the licence of both print and manuscript. If the delay caused by this had been sufficiently protracted, the printing might have run on into the following year, in which case, the title page being already printed, all that could be done was to insert an extra I. Though the Ste. Geneviève 1572 copy contains the same licence as the others that creates no difficulty, for it is simply a copy which has escaped having the date altered.

All this is mere speculation, for there may have been no difficulty about the licence at all. Plenty of other reasons suggest themselves : there may have been a strike in the printing office, or there may have been a fire, or the type might have been required in a hurry for another book, and Stephanus Alexandrinus would have to wait, or political disturbances may have hindered the printer. I have looked in the chronologies to see if Padua was the scene of any commotion in 1572, but without success. Very likely it was none of these, and the only reason for changing the date was to pass off a year-old book as newly issued from the press ; or perhaps there was a defect which involved the cancelling of a leaf or sheet. To test this would involve a word-for-word comparison of a 1573 copy with that of 1572. This I have not had an opportunity of doing, and I doubt if there would be any result.

I frankly admit my inability at present to set this question at rest, and I must leave it over for future enquiry.

20. My conclusion, in the meantime, is this :—

Pizimenti's translation was *begun* to be printed at Padua in 1572. The first portion of this reached Cologne before March 1st, 1572, in time to be added to Birckmann's Mizaldus. The Padua edition was finished in 1572, or possibly not till 1573. At any rate, in the majority of copies the date 1572 of the title page (which seems to have been printed at once as part of the first sheet) was changed to 1573.

In 1573 Birckmann printed a new edition, and in 1574 the rest of it was issued with altered date only.

The book then disappeared till 1717, when it was printed in Latin at Nürnberg.

Kopp reprinted the translation of Democritus only in 1869.

Finally, Berthelot printed the Greek text, for the first time, in 1888.

I have seen all these editions. If I should come across the edition of Rome, 1570, or the German translation of 1717, I shall, I hope, be able to describe them to the Society, for then the list would be complete The Roman edition is very doubtful ; I do not think there is one. The German translation is, of course, possible; up to the present I have met with no copy, and the results of all my investigations are antagonistic to it.

21. I never anticipated that the list should extend as it has done. When the excessive and almost unaccountable rarity of every one of the editions is considered, it was improbable that they should have been, after all, so attainable as they have proved to be. Of the different copies enumerated in § 9 I have seen all except Nos. 6, 9, 10, and 11.

I am only too glad, at this resting-place in the investigation, to acknowledge with my best thanks the help and goodwill I have received from the librarians of the different libraries at home and on the continent, and from personal friends, without which this investigation could not have been made so complete even as it is.

[*October* 1, 1892.—Since the preceding was written I have ascertained that in the Bibliothèque Mazarine at Paris there is a copy of an edition of Democritus *De Arte Magna*, by Pizimenti, printed at Padua in 1570, in 4°. I have not as yet seen it, and am therefore unable to say what it contains, or what light it may throw on the points that are still doubtful. There is no mention anywhere of a Padua edition of this date, for though Conring gives the date 1570, the place he specifies is Rome. Hitherto I have been doubtful about Conring's statement, but the undoubted existence of a Padua edition of 1570 makes the possibility of an edition printed at Rome in the same year much greater than before. I hope before long to lay before the Society the results of my examination of this quite unforeseen addition to the material of the research.]

ERRATUM.

§ 21, line 6, *for* Nos. 6, 9, 10, and 11, *read* Nos. 7, 10, 11, and 12.

[redacted]

Philosophical Society of Glasgow.

1893-94.

ON THE FIRST EDITION

OF THE

CHEMICAL WRITINGS

OF

DEMOCRITUS AND SYNESIUS.

PART IV.

BY

PROFESSOR JOHN FERGUSON, LL.D., F.S.A., F.C.S.,

PRESIDENT OF THE SOCIETY.

GLASGOW:

PRINTED BY ROBERT ANDERSON, 22 ANN STREET.

[FROM THE *PROCEEDINGS* OF THE PHILOSOPHICAL SOCIETY OF GLASGOW.]

On the First Edition of the Chemical Writings of Democritus and Synesius. Part IV. By Professor JOHN FERGUSON, LL.D., F.S.A., F.C.S., President of the Society.

[Read before the Society, December 13th, 1893.]

1. Two sessions ago, on November 18th, 1891,[1] I submitted to the Society complete proof that the edition of the works of Democritus and others by Pizimenti, apparently published at Padua in 1573, was originally dated 1572, and that the date had been subsequently altered by the insertion of an additional figure I. Photo-facsimiles of the title-pages of three 1573 copies were sufficient of themselves to have established this fact; but there was, over and above, the direct evidence of the copy actually dated 1572, in the Bibliothèque Ste. Geneviève—after which there was nothing more to say.

2. It was not settled, however, whether or not there was a previous edition. Later on, I was startled and interested by being told "that in the Bibliothèque Mazarine at Paris there is a copy of an edition of Democritus *De Arte Magna*, by Pizimenti, printed at Padua in 1570, in 4°," and to the paper I added a supplementary note with that information, on October 1st, 1892.[2] This, as I then observed, was quite an unlooked-for enlargement of the list of editions, for, though one printed at Rome in 1570 had been mentioned by Conring, there was no allusion anywhere to one printed at Padua in that year. There was no alternative, however, but to accept the statement as I received it, and to express the hope, as I then did, of laying before the Society the results of my inquiries about this hitherto unknown edition, which I am now able to do.

3. In February last I obtained a photograph of the title-page and a description of the copy in the Mazarine Library. The photograph, which I have had printed, like the others, tells its own story, the *dénouement* of which could not well be more

---

[1] *Proceedings* of the Philosophical Society of Glasgow, 1892, Vol. XXIII., p. 153.

[2] *Ibid.*, p. 167.

tantalising, for just the most important part of all, the date, is
missing. Comparison, however, with the other title-pages leaves
no doubt that this is nothing but another copy of the 1572-73
edition, which is confirmed by a collation of the book itself.
From the description accompanying the photograph[1] the following
extracts give all necessary information. In his letter M. J.
Havet styles it correctly "the so-called Democritus of 1570 in
the bibliothèque Mazarine, vol. 27,481. As may be seen," he
adds, "the lower part of the leaf is torn out, leaving the year
uncertain; the sole authority for supposing this to be 1570 is the
entry in the manuscript catalogue of the Mazarine, compiled in
the XVIIIth century. But if your friend will take the trouble
to compare this photo with the edition of 1573 (of which we have
a copy in the National Library, R. 33395), he will easily convince
himself that it is the same book. The number of pages, paging,
signatures, &c., are the same. From this we can, I think, safely
infer that the entry in the Mazarine Catalogue is erroneous, and
that the edition of Padua 1570 never existed."

I myself have not the smallest doubt that the date in the
Mazarine Catalogue is an error, and that this is a copy of the
1572-73 edition. It so happens that I have already given[2] a
facsimile of the copy referred to (Bibl. Nat., R. 33395), and
comparison will show identity, even to the correction of the initial
'I' to 'A' in "Abderita,' and to the defect in the lower part of
the initial 'P' in 'Patavii.' From the arrangement of the
figures it is quite obvious that the date could not have been
MDLXX., if they were placed symmetrically below "Patavii,"
and in the centre of the title. Whether, however, this was an
original unaltered copy, like that in the Ste. Geneviève Library, or
an amended one, like all the rest, it is impossible to decide; the
crucial test, unfortunately, cannot be applied.

I think we may infer that this was an imperfect copy when it
was catalogued. If it had been unmutilated, then the date in the
catalogue would have been either 1572 or 1573; but, as this
guidance was wanting, the cataloguer had to fall back on internal
evidence, and, finding Pizimenti's dedication dated 1570, he
assumed that to be the date of the printed volume. One is

---

[1] For both I am indebted to J. Y. W. Macalister, Esq., F.S.A., who
procured them from the late M. J. Havet, of Paris.

[2] In Part III., § 5, *Proceedings*, Vol. XXIII., p. 154.

DEMOCRITVS

ABDERITA
DE ARTE
MAGNA.

Siue de rebus naturalibus.

Nec non Synesii,& Pelagii , & Stephani Alexandrini, & Michaelis Pselli in eundem commentaria.

Dominico Pizimentio Vibonensi
Interprete.

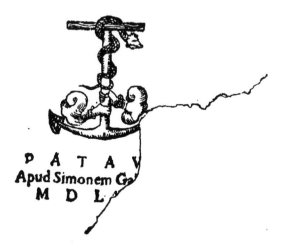

PATAV
Apud Simonem Ga
M D L

DEMOCRITVS

ABDERITA

DE ARTE

MAGNA,

Siue de rebus naturalibus.

Nec non Synesii, & Pelagii, & Stephani Alexandrini, & Michaelis Psel.
li in enndem commentaria.

Dominico Pizimentio Vibonensi
Interprete.

PATAVII
Apud Simonem Galignanum
M D LXXIII.

hardly justified in saying, from the exact similarity of this and the Bibliothèque Nationale copy, that a Padua edition of 1570 never existed, but the existence of any edition dated 1570 is certainly rendered less and less probable, when every fresh copy that is examined proves to be dated 1572, or usually 1573. Anyhow, no 1570 copy is as yet forthcoming.

4. The Mazarine copy is not the only one to be added to the list; there is another, dated 1573, in the Library of St. Mark at Venice. For an account of this copy, with a tracing of the title-page, I am indebted to Sign. Mario Girardi, Librarian of the Royal University of Padua, who wrote me a letter on the subject a year ago, on December 26th, 1892. Though a tracing cannot be quite so exact as a photograph, I have had it reproduced, for it is sufficient to illustrate the alteration of the initial of ABDERITA, the alteration of the date by the insertion of a I, and the identity of the title-page in all respects with the others.

This copy is the fourth in a volume of pamphlets, and is numbered 44659. Comparison of it with the account given by me in Part III., § 14 (a copy of which had been sent to Sign. Girardi), showed that the book is exactly similar to the Cambridge copy, and, therefore, also to the copy described below in § 11.

5. With regard to the title-page, Sign. Girardi draws attention to the fact that the initial A in Abderita occupies a position similar to that in the Bibliothèque Nationale copy, which, as will be seen from the facsimiles, is different from that in the Cambridge and Göttingen copies. In the latter two the corrected A covers the original I, and falls nearly under the E in Democritus, whereas in the Paris and Venice copies the A comes close to the B, and is placed nearly under the M of Democritus. The Venice copy has also a spot of ink where the I has been, and the letter can be traced through it, so that in this copy the I has been attempted to be cancelled, and the A has been put in separately, whereas in the Cambridge and Göttingen copies the I has been obscured by having the A put on the top of it. As to the position of the middle figure I in the date, it resembles the Göttingen copy, and not those of Cambridge and the Bibliothèque Nationale.

6. As not infrequently happens that the place where a book was printed retains no example of it, so it is here. Padua possesses no copy of this book that first appeared in it. There is, however, another copy, dated 1573, in the Biblioteca Comunale of Verona. Of the title-page of this copy I am able to give a facsimile from a

photograph by R. Lotze, of Verona. The points to be observed
are, as usual, the initial A of ABDERITA, and its position under
the E of DEMOCRITUS, and the position of the inserted I in
the date. In this instance it is placed rather to one side, so
that this particular example corresponds with the Cambridge
University and Bibliothèque Nationale copies.

7. To the evidence already adduced that the edition of 1572-73
is the first of this book, there may be added, if such be needed, the
statement of an author whom I was unable to quote in my previous
paper (Part III., § 10). Philip Labbe, in his very rare book,[1]
Nova Bibliotheca MSS. Librorum, Paris, 1653, 4°, p. 128, mentions
the fact that the treatise of Psellus on the confection of gold,
addressed to Michaël Cerularius, was translated by Pizimenti, and
published along with Democritus Abderita, Synesius, Pelagius
and Stephanus Alexandrinus De Magna et Sacra Arte, at Padua,
by Simon Galignanus, in 1572, in 8vo. This is an earlier allusion
to this edition than any I have hitherto encountered. The rarity
of Pizimenti's book must have been great even two hundred and
fifty years ago, for it remained unknown to Reinesius when he
was describing the Altenburg-Gotha[2] manuscript of the Greek
alchemists, and when he wrote the tract on the same topic which
Fabricius printed afterwards in 1724.[3] It is remarkable that, in
this account by Labbe, Psellus' tract is said to be dedicated to
Michaël Cerularius, whereas in the printed edition of 1573 it is
dedicated to Xiphilinus, the Patriarch. What was the reason for
this change does not appear. It is quite certain, however, that in
a manuscript of the tract in Greek, preserved in the Vatican, the
dedication is to Cerularius.[4]

---

[1] There is no copy in the British Museum, but I have got it in the
University Library at Cambridge. Sign. Girardi, who refers to this book,
says that he has not had access to a copy of it.

[2] *Variae Lectiones*, Altenburg, 1640.

[3] Fabricius, *Bibliotheca Graeca*, Hamburgi, 1724, XII.

[4] Henricus Stevenson, *Codices Manuscripti Palatini Graeci Bibliothecae
Vaticanae descripti.* Romae Ex Typographeo Vaticano MDCCCLXXXV. 4°,
p. 270 :—

*415. Chart. in 8, Saec. XV exeuntis. . . .

    Michaëlis Pselli (iunioris, Tractatus) Περὶ χρυσοποιίας, seu de
auri conficiendi ratione, ad Michaëlem (Cerularium), Patriarcham
(C Politanum). Inc. Ὁρᾷς, ὁ ἐμὸς δυνάστης, ὅ με ποιεῖς f. 35.

Pizimenti's translation begins (f. 65 *recto*) : Vides ò domine quidnam facis
meus dynastes, & animi mei tyrannis?

DEMOCRITVS
ABDERITA
DE ARTE
MAGNA.

Siue de rebus naturalibus.

Nec non Synesii, & Pelagii, & Stephani Alexandrini, & Michaelis Pselli in eundem commentaria.

Dominico Pizimentio Vibonense
Interprete.

PATAVII
Apud Simonem Galignanum
M D LXXIII.

8. To those who have quoted the 1572 and 1574 reprints appended to the Cologne edition of Mizaldus must be added Eloy.[1] Under "Democrite," he refers to the Greek MSS. bearing his name which exist in the Library at the Louvre, but which were supposed to be spurious, and then he quotes from Vander Linden Mizaldus' *Memorabilia,* with Democritus, Synesius, and Pelagius appended, Coloniæ, 1574, and a Greek MS. at Leyden of the *Phyſicorum & Myſticorum Liber cum Syneſii & Stephani Commentariis.* In a later edition[2] he says of this MS. : "Il étoit à Leyde parmi les Manuſcrits de la Bibliotheque de *Jean Elichmann,* ſavant Médecin de cette Ville." Then he quotes the title of Pizimenti's tract, and adds : "Ou trouve ce Livre dans le Recueil d' *Antoine Mizauld,* qui a paru à Cologne en 1572, *in*-12, & en 1574, *in*-16, ſous le titre de *Memorabilium, ſive, Arcanorum omnis generis Centuriæ novem.*

9. In Part III., § 12, a certain amount of evidence has been adduced which throws strong doubt upon the existence of a German translation of 1717. If anything more were wanted, it can be got in a book which I knew, but omitted to quote on that occasion. Reference was made to three works by Friedrich Roth-Scholtz, but there ought to have been added a fourth, his *Deutsches Theatrum Chemicum,* Nürnberg, 1728-32. In his preface to the third and last volume, 1732, he gives a list of chemical works which he had published between 1717 and 1732. On p. 23 occurs the following :—

XIII.—Democritvs, *Abderyta Græcus,* de Rebus Sacris Naturalibus & Myſticis ; cum Notis Synesii & Pelagii. 8. Norimbergæ, apud Hæredes Joh. Dan. Tauberi. 1717.

Again, on p. 25 :—

XVIII.—Des vortrefflichen Abts Synesii, aus Griechenland, Chymiſche Schrifften, von dem gebenedeyten Stein der Weisen und deſſen Bereitung; wie ſolche ehemahls aus der Kayferlichen Bibliothec ſind communiciret, nun aber zum Druck befördert worden, durch Friederich Roth-Scholtzen, Herrenſtad. Silef. 8. Nürnberg, bey Joh. Dan. Taubers ſeel. Erben. 1718.

At the end of this volume, in order to fill a few blank leaves, Roth-Scholtz adds a list of old and new chemical books

---

[1] M. F. J. Eloy, *Dictionnaire Historique de la Médicine,* Liége & Francfort en Foire, 1755, 2 Tomes, 8vo. I., p. 276.

[2] *Dictionnaire Historique de la Médecine, Ancienne et Moderne.* Mons, 1778, 4 Tomes, 4°. Tome II., p. 20.

to be had at a cheap rate from Johann Daniel Tauber's heirs in Nürnberg. Among others is the following, p. 959 :—

> Democritus Abderyta Græcus de Rebus Sacris Naturalibus & Myfticis, cum Notis Synefii & Pelagii, Tumba Semirandis (*sic*) Hermeticæ (*sic*) Sigillatæ quam fi Sapiens aperuerit, non Cyrus, Ambitiofus, Avarus 8. Norimbergæ, 1717.

This last entry is both imperfect and inaccurate, as can be seen by referring to Part I., § 13. That, however, does not concern us, because the chief reason for which I quote these notices is to show the entire absence in them, as in the earlier ones, of reference to a *German* translation of Democritus, Synesius & Pelagius, dated 1717. The work ascribed to the Abt Synesius is, as I pointed out in Part I., §§ 16, 17, and in the Postscript to that Part, § 3, quite different from the commentary by Synesius on Democritus.

If, therefore, there was such an edition, it was not•edited by Roth-Scholtz, and it was not published by Tauber's heirs, and, therefore, my opinion is stronger than ever that there is no edition in German of 1717, and that Dufresnoy and Schmieder, who are the sole authorities for it, are both in error.

10. This part of the subject has now been exhausted. Other copies, dated 1572 or 1573, as may be, are doubtless still to find, but, unless they have manuscript notes, they cannot be expected to add anything to what is now known about the history of the book.

My opinion further is, that an edition of 1570 and the German translation of 1717 must be finally given up. The evidence for their existence is so small and feeble, it rests on such defective authority, and can be so easily overturned, whereas the evidence against their existence is so abundant and strong, becoming more and more conclusive with every new discovery, that nothing except actual copies of both would convince me now that such editions were produced. Such evidence, I think, will never be forthcoming, and, therefore, it may be affirmed with all certainty that the first edition of Pizimenti's work is that dated 1572-1573.

11. Had I planned a conclusion to this series of researches, which have now extended from November, 1884, to the present time, I could not have got one more appropriate than that which has spontaneously offered itself to me. On the 28th of November last, just a fortnight ago, a copy of the book, about which so much has been written during the past three hundred years, came

DEMOCRITVS

ABDERITA
DE ARTE
MAGNA,

Siue de rebus naturalibus.

Nec non Synefii, & Pelagii, & Stephani Alexandrini, & Michaelis Pfel-
li in eundem commentaria.

Dominico Pizimentio Vibonensi
Interprete.

P A T A V I I
Apud Simonem Galignanum
M D L X X I I I.

into my possession, and I have brought it to-night for exhibition. All the copies of this edition which I have quoted are in public libraries. This is an unknown copy, and bears no evidence of the source from which it has come. I have had the title-page photographed and printed for comparison with the others. In this, as in the Cambridge and Göttingen copies, the initial A in Abderita is larger than the other letters, and it is printed over the original I, though not so as to altogether conceal it, and it falls under the E in Democritus. The added I in the date, like that in the Göttingen and Venice copies, is placed about half-way between the other two. It is, as in all the others, a shade smaller in size, and in this particular copy it proclaims itself as an obvious addition, by being less clearly printed than the rest.

12. After all is said, the book is not much to look at, and some wonder may be excited as to why it should have attracted so much notice. The answer is obvious : because it is the first attempt to make known the oldest views promulgated on the *sacred art, the great art,* on *alchemy,* as it was termed at a much later date, after the Arabian chemists had taken it up. It is, in short, the first edition of the oldest writing on Chemistry. It is possessed, therefore, of supreme historical importance as the translation of a document that emanated from one who may have lived as early as the second century A.D., and certainly not later than the fourth century.

Even though the Latin text be now easily available in Kopp's reprint, and the Greek text in Berthelot's edition, that in no way diminishes the value of Pizimenti's version as a historical authority. Kopp reprinted Democritus only; Birckmann reprinted Democritus, Synesius and Pelagius; so that for Stephanus Alexandrinus and Psellus, recourse must still be had to the Padua edition. Moreover, as Pizimenti's version was made from a MS. which came from Corfu, and not from the St. Mark MS., which is the basis of Berthelot's edition, it serves to show how far the two MSS. agreed with one another. Besides, Pizimenti, living at a time when the belief in alchemy and in the possibility of transmutation was a genuine one, viewed the treatises he translated in a very different way from what could be done at the present time by any editor or historian however unbiassed, however anxious to deal fairly with these older conceptions and theories. To Pizimenti alchemy was a vital motive and factor; to the modern student it is a past finished fact.

13. There is also the interest attaching to the book itself, its remarkable rarity, and its history. Certain not unprofitable general considerations can be drawn from even the bibliography of this book. In 1867 Dr. Kopp knew of only one copy of Pizimenti's translation, which he got after much seeking. Books so rare as that are sometimes called unique, and their value is naturally to a certain extent enhanced thereby. In the course of this research ten copies have been mentioned, and there may be, probably there are, more. It is never safe to assert, and it is all but impossible to prove, that of the edition of a book published in the ordinary way the one copy that is *known* is *unique*. Of books believed to be so, and described in important catalogues as such, it has happened that other copies have been discovered which have dispelled that belief.

The course of the enquiry further shows how very hard it is, in the absence of definite data, to determine by mere speculation and inference a matter of fact so apparently simple as the date of a book. The difficulty, perhaps, is not so much in fixing the year as in detecting and nullifying the errors of those who thought they knew it, but did not, and of those who adopted the errors of others without either thinking or criticism. But if such errors have been made as to the date of an obscure book, and the correction and dispelling of them involves so much investigation and examination of minute detail, what certainty can be felt about the accuracy of much that passes current for ancient history, and for all that passes for modern or newspaper history, which is nothing but fanciful narrative from unsifted data—that is, no data at all? So one bibliography supersedes another because it is more accurate; one historian pushes others from their stools because he has taken more trouble with the facts, because his errors are less abundant.

14. The most annoying circumstance connected with the whole enquiry is the unpardonable stupidity of Fra. Massimiano da Crema, *Inquisitor Paduœ.* When he admits that he saw the book, partly in print and partly in manuscript, and yet leaves this all-important statement without a date, which would have been invaluable for the history of the book for all time coming, his incapacity for the post he held stands self-revealed. Had he dated his permit, we might have had a clue to the cause of the alteration of the year; to the time when the material for the Cologne reprint was despatched; to the cause of the licence being received after the printing was

begun. We might have known whether the book of 83 leaves, partly in print, which he mentions, was this edition, begun in 1572, or another earlier one. There is nothing for it but to lament the want of this date, and wish that fate could deliver the *Inquisitor* over to us for one brief, but for him very bad, quarter of an hour. May one hope that, for leaving his work in this world undated, the punishment he is deservedly undergoing is, as regards its conclusion, in the same condition?

15. It seems fitting now to give, as on former occasions, a list of all the copies of the different editions, knowledge of which has accumulated during the course of my enquiries :—

1893 LIST.

1.	Padua, 1572, ...	...	Bibliothèque Ste. Geneviève, Paris.
2.	Cologne, 1572, ...	...	Hunterian Library, ⎫
3.	,, ,, ...	...	University Library, ⎬ Glasgow.
4.	,, ,, ...	...	University Library, Cambridge.
5.	,, ,, ...	...	New College, Oxford.
6.	,, ,, ...	...	Trinity College, Cambridge.
7.	,, ,, ...	...	Copy seen by Dr. Kopp.
8.	Padua, 1573, ...	...	University Library, Cambridge.
9.	,, ,, ...	...	Bibliothèque Nationale.
10.	,, ,, ...	...	University Library, Göttingen.
11.	,, ,, ...	...	Barberini Library, ⎫ Rome.
12.	,, ,, ...	...	,, ,, ⎭
13.	,, ,, ...	...	Biblioteca Di S. Marco, Venice.
14.	,, ,, ...	...	Biblioteca Comunale, Verona.
15.	,, ,, ...	...	Professor Ferguson's copy.
16.	,, 1572-73,...	...	Bibliothèque Mazarine, Paris.
17.	Cologne, 1573, ...	...	British Museum.
18.	,, 1574, ...	...	University Library, Cambridge.
19.	,, ,, ...	...	University Library, Aberdeen.
20.	Nürnberg, 1717,	...	Young Collection, Glasgow.
21.	Braunschweig, 1869,	...	Reprint in Kopp's Beiträge.
22.	Paris, 1888, ...	...	Berthelot's Greek edition.

16. It is to myself, after all I have had to say and to argue, a most satisfactory result that at the very end I can bring before the Society a copy of this exceedingly rare book—so far as I know, the only one in Scotland, and, with the exception of the Cambridge one, the only one in Britain—and in so doing to express my belief that this part of the subject is at last concluded.

[*Note.*—Brussels, 28th September, 1894.—Since the preceding was printed I have seen once more the copy at the Ste. Geneviève

Library at Paris, and hope to be able to complete the series of
facsimiles by giving one of the sole surviving 1572 title-page.
This, however, must be done in a supplement.]

Erratum in Part III., *Proceedings*, Vol. XXIII.
§ 16, line 8—*for* non in ho trovato, *read* non ui ho trovato.

Philosophical Society of Glasgow.

1893-94.

JOHN FERGUSON, LL.D., F.R.S.E., F.C.S.,

Professor of Chemistry in the University of Glasgow,

ON THE

FIRST EDITION OF THE CHEMICAL WRITINGS OF DEMOCRITUS AND SYNESIUS.

POSTSCRIPT TO PART IV.

DEMOCRITVS
ABDERITA.
DE ARTE
MAGNA,

Siue de rebus naturalibus.

Nec non Synesii, & Pelagii, & Stephani Alexandrini, & Michaelis Pselli in eundem commentaria.

Dominico Pizimentio Vibonensi
Interprete.

PATAVII
Apud Simonem Galignanum
M D L X X I I.

[FROM THE *PROCEEDINGS* OF THE PHILOSOPHICAL SOCIETY OF GLASGOW.]

On the First Edition of the Chemical Writings of Democritus and Synesius. By Professor FERGUSON.

POSTSCRIPT TO PART IV.

1. When I saw M. Dujardin, the distinguished photo-artist, in Paris last month, he undertook to send me a negative of the unique copy of Democritus by Pizimenti, in the Bibliothèque Ste. Geneviève. Having now received it, I am able to give a reproduction of it as the most important addition that I can make to what has been already said.

2. There are two points specially to be noticed. The first is the date: MDLXXII. This is the only copy of the book I have met with having this date, although others possibly exist without having attracted attention. All other copies which I have seen have had the date altered to MDLXXIII., by the subsequent insertion of an additional figure I.

The second point is the initial A of ABDERITA. In all copies except this one, the correction of the original misprint, IBDERITA, has been effected by means of a printed A. In this copy, however, the alteration has been done with the pen. To print the correction, therefore, was probably an after-thought, and may have been carried out at the same time as the alteration of the date. If another copy dated MDLXXII. be found, in all probability the original misprint IBDERITA will either have been left unaltered, or corrected by hand as in the present copy. If this inference be correct, then it may be concluded that the date which has been torn away from the copy in the Mazarine Library (see Part IV., § 3, and the facsimile) had been changed to MDLXXIII. like the others, because the initial I has been *reprinted* A, and not altered by hand. This is an entirely new aspect of the subject, which did not occur to me till I re-examined the Ste. Geneviève copy. It can be dealt with only by comparison of copies dated MDLXXII., and if in any of these there is a *printed* correction of I to A, the argument necessarily falls to the ground. I believe, however, that, when the date has not been changed, the correction of I to A will be in manuscript, if made at all.

3. It is with much satisfaction that I am able to present this facsimile to the Society, for, as I have repeatedly said, it confirms all the theories and arguments which I had put forward as to the original date of the book, before I had seen it. See particularly Part I., 1884, § 10; Part II., 1890, § 12, and postscript; Part III., 1891, §§ 7, 8.

4. Reuvens,[1] speaking of the Greek alchemical MSS., mentions the fact that a small part of the original texts had been printed by Fabricius, Ducange, d'Orville, and Bernard, and in Latin by Pizimentius. He adds :—

,, Mais toujours est-il vrai de dire que la plupart des traités en question sont restés inédits, d'autant plus que même la traduction de Pizimentius [1573] est presque introuvable, et que d'ailleurs, pour l'étude approfondie de cette matière, il est indispensable de posséder les textes grecs originaux, que cet éditeur n' a pas joints à sa traduction."

Reuvens is quite correct about the necessity of basing the study of the subject upon the original texts, and this can now be done in an edition, the appearance of which would have gratified not only Reuvens, but Beckmann, Borrichius, Leo Allatius, and others who were deeply interested in the early history of the science.

Sixty years ago Pizimenti's little volume was "almost not to be got." Those who have followed the inquiry will, I think, admit that this account of Pizimenti's book is still strictly true.

5. As a proof that no subject ever really comes to an end, a reference which is new may be given.

In the *Catalogue des Manuscrits Grecs des Bibliothèques de Suisse*, Leipzig, Otto Harrassowitz, 1886, 8°, Henri Omont quotes a MS. in the Bibliothèque de la Ville, at Berne. It is No. 113 in his list, and apparently No. 579 of the Berne list, and it is of the XV.-XVI. century, written on paper. Of this MS. folios 41-47, in the hand of Ange Vergèce, contain the following :—

"Synesii philosophi liber ad Dioscurum de libro Democriti. Τῆς πεμφθείσης μοι ἐπιστολῆς . . . "

It is evidently an unknown copy of the Commentary of Synesius upon Democritus addressed to Dioscurus. Comparison with

---

[1] *Lettres à M. Letronne . . . Sur les Papyrus Bilingues et Grecs, . . . du Musée d'antiquités de l'Université de Leide*, Leide, 1830, 4to. Troisième Lettre, p. 71.

other MSS. alone would show which of those earlier than itself it most resembled.

The text of this Epistle, as it exists in the St. Mark MS., will be found in Berthelot's edition, Paris, 1888, volume containing the Greek text, p. 57. Pizimenti's version begins on f. 11 *verso*:—

" Epistolam tuam ad me missam de diuini Democriti libello non negligenter accepi, . . . "

The Berne MS. was not known to Dr. Kopp when he drew up his account of the Greek Alchemical MSS. (see *Beiträge zur Geschichte der Chemie*, Braunschweig, 1869 ; and my Address to the Chemical Section of the Philosophical Society, *Proceedings*, 1876-77, vol. X., pp. 373-74), and the above is the only notice of it which I have observed.

GLASGOW, *25th October, 1894.*

Erratum in Part II., § 10, line 15, *for* Birckmann *read* Beckmann.

CPSIA information can be obtained
at www.ICGtesting.com
Printed in the USA
LVHW081458230721
693510LV00011B/785